Where The Dust Never
Settles

Where The Dust Never Settles

Mostly Truthful Tales of Hectic Family Life

Tim Herrera

Writers Club Press

San Jose New York Lincoln Shanghai

Where The Dust Never Settles
Mostly Truthful Tales of Hectic Family Life

Writers Club Press
an imprint of iUniverse, Inc.

For information address:
iUniverse, Inc.
5220 S. 16th St., Suite 200
Lincoln, NE 68512
www.iuniverse.com

ISBN: 0-595-21452-5

Printed in the United States of America

WHAT PEOPLE ARE SAYING ABOUT WHERE THE DUST NEVER SETTLES

"WHERE THE DUST NEVER SETTLES is a pleasant journey into one father's experience of wearing the badge of honor known as 'Dad.'"

Cathy Morelli, syndicated columnist, PEAKS AND VALLEYS and author of THE FLYING NUN, THE PIZZA MAN AND ME.

"WHERE THE DUST NEVER SETTLES dives right into the fun mayhem of everyday life with kids. Tim Herrera is like Dave Barry, sharing wit and wisecracks on topics as universal as buying a cell phone to the challenges of back-to-school season. He's written a comical view of a Dad's view of the trials and joys of parenthood."

Linda Singleton, author of the YA cloning series, REGENERATION.

"Tim Herrera deals with true-to-life situations with warm wit and a wry sense of humor. If you have children, this book is a must. It's a fun read that's difficult to put down."

Debbie Farmer, syndicated humor columnist and author of LIFE IN THE FAST FOOD LANE

"Tim Herrera captures family life in a nutshell. As a father of four children he has developed a required sense of humor. His collection of stories supply desperately needed laughs after a stressful day."

Wendy Layne, Family Humor Columnist

"As a mother of three, I truly appreciate the humor Tim Herrera reminds us of in the parenting world."

Kellei Hennessey Founder, THE BABY FOUNDATION

DEDICATION

To my wife Carol who helps me believe that most things are possible and that anything that appears to be impossible should not be avoided.

CONTENTS

INTRODUCTION

One white Nike basketball shoe with red stripes, children's size six, sits in the middle of the living room floor. The shoe's partner is somewhere within the walls of our two-story house, but that's the best we can narrow down the location for now. The other shoe could be in the garage beneath the foosball table. Then again it might be behind the desk in the master bedroom because that's just as logical of a place for a white Nike basketball shoe with red stripes, children's size six, as any place else.

Come to think of it…if we looked in the corner under the stack of empty videocassette boxes, the ones we told the kids to refill with the proper videos, the shoe might be under there.

No, wait a minute. Missing homework projects are always hiding under the video boxes. Everyone knows that. What was I thinking?

The white Nike is probably trapped under that heap of naked Barbies upstairs. You know the stack of dolls right next to the pile of dirty laundry that someone forgot to deposit in the hamper, but probably couldn't because there wasn't a forklift available.

This is what it's always like living in a place "Where The Dust Never Settles." With four kids wreaking havoc, two parents struggling to maintain order and one dog just trying to stay out of the way, the home is a place of perpetual motion. And as long as the kids are still living at home and eating the food you buy and wetting the beds you're still trying to pay for and leaving everything they own in a spot that guarantees they'll never find anything, the dust will never settle.

And that's just fine. It's something to be savored.

This book is about enjoying the craziness that goes along with a household jam-packed with so much frenzy that it is oozing out the windows.

Sometimes as parents, we are too caught up in trying to pay the bills on time, getting everyone to soccer practice on time, making the parent/teacher conference on time and getting the kids to eat something that doesn't get handed to you by some teenager wearing a headset on the other side of a drive through window. Sometimes we get so caught up in all that junk that we forget to laugh at what's funny and treasure the moments that make us cry.

I hope this book will help with that.

Whether it's the usual hectic morning before school, the pains associated with listening to the children learn a musical instrument or you trying your best to learn the "slanguage" that the kids have acquired, there's always something within those events to laugh at and enjoy. When the kids are all gone and you're walking from empty bedroom to empty bedroom, you're going to hear all the sounds that made you cackle and hopefully not the ones that made you pull your hair out.

"Where The Dust Never Settles: Mostly Truthful Tales of Hectic Family Life" is designed for all the parents who need to be reminded that it's the fury of family life that makes things fun. It's the unpredictability of family life that gives it life.

And hopefully, by the time you've finished reading this book, we will have found the elusive white Nike. Wish us luck!

LET'S GET BUSY

"Success usually comes to those who are too busy to be look-ing for it."

Henry David Thoreau

"The way I see it, you got two choices. You either gotta get busy livin'…or get busy dyin'."

Shawshank Redemption by Stephen King

Armageddon In The A.M.

It's serene at first, like the first few moments after a light rain. The silence is enough to lull the crickets to sleep. Everything is still and right with the world and you feel at peace.

I'm talking about that part in the day when you step out onto the front porch to snatch the morning paper before the sprinklers sprout and squirt, while the steam rises from your first cup of coffee. A jogger trots by, waves and sidesteps the bicycle helmet one of the cute, yet slightly irresponsible neighborhood kids left on the sidewalk. You let the dog out to take care of business, and spy some bleary-eyed neighbor—who leaves for work before you do—sleepily rooting around in his pockets for the car keys.

That's the tranquil time of the day and you know that it's not going to last.

Just when you feel at ease, when all is right in your little world, there's a tiny voice in the back of your head telling you that the "tornado" is about to strike. It's the part of the day when the peacefulness shatters into a million pieces. It's the part of the day when you have to pry the kids out of bed and get them ready for school and get yourself ready for work.

It is Armageddon in the a.m.

It starts with an alarm clock. It's usually one of theirs, one of the kids. It just keeps buzzing because they're in a coma-like sleep that only ice water can crack.

No one budges. The cyclone simmers.

"GET UP! YOU'RE ALL GOING TO BE LATE!" shouts one of us from the walk-in closet while the other hops from bedroom to bedroom ripping warm covers off slumbering children.

Eventually, they all begin to stir, all at their own pace. They reluctantly roll out of bed to mechanically reach for underwear, socks and tennis shoes.

3

The twister picks up speed.

"WHO'S PACKING AND WHO'S BUYING LUNCH TODAY?"

The storm builds. The children yank on their pants and shirts. They stuff their backpacks with crumpled homework papers that may or may not be legible, and you hope you have time to check their assignments before they leave for school.

"WE ARE RUNNING OUT OF TIME! GET A MOVE ON!"

A rush of small feet pounds the stairs and once they all reach the kitchen the tornado is in full swing. Anyone not wishing to dare risk injury must get out of the way or face the consequences.

"I want toaster waffles, but not the strawberry kind. I want the plain kind and with butter on both sides."

"Mom, sign this permission slip for a field trip. I need all my medical information on it and twenty-dollars too."

"You know, I think I was supposed to bring poster board to school for a group project. Dad, is Staples open now?"

The storm in the house continues to grow as assignment sheets begin to float in the air, small hands hurriedly open cupboards to pluck boxes of cereal from the shelves. The light fixture hanging above the breakfast table starts to sway in the breeze created by the commotion of the morning rush.

It's time to hang onto the wall to steady yourselves!

The toaster ejects slightly burned waffles. A small stream of orange juice mysteriously appears on the kitchen table and no one is responsible for the mess. One child cries about the unfairness of eating another peanut butter and jelly sandwich for lunch. Another child races around looking for the library book that is past due.

In a flash, the twister reaches full force.

"WE HAVE TO GO…NOW!"

With arms flailing to fit into coat sleeves, we all hurry to the car. The front door bursts open and then slams shut. Inside the house, papers slowly drift onto the carpet in a gentle swirling movement. The hanging light stops swaying and the bulb we all forgot to turn off highlights the trickle of sticky juice that no one spilled and everyone forgot to clean up. Sensing that the storm has passed, the dog slinks out from behind the couch to survey the damage, and to scrounge around for any morsels of food left within a snout's reach.

The cyclone has passed, but is guaranteed to return within twenty-four hours.

The house is at peace again, with no one but the pooch left to enjoy the solitude.

Ground Meat And Ketchup, Stupid

All I wanted was a simple recipe for sloppy joes. The ground meat had already defrosted in a big plastic bowl, looking like a lump of clay waiting to be molded into something fantastic, or at least edible. The tater tots were within reach. Cut up some fruit and there you have it…a quick weeknight meal. But where was that darned index card with the ingredients jotted down in my wife's orderly handwriting? Without that 3x5 card I was sunk and the meat was destined for a future as hamburger patties, something the kids had for dinner just a few days before. I could already hear their whining ringing inside my head.

My wife was working and I was in charge of the meal. In fact, I was in charge of most of the meals that week and the week before. I took vacation time to "hang out" with the kids during their summer break while my wife tended to her teaching duties inside her kindergarten classroom.

"It'll be good for you to spend this time with the kids," my wife said. "They'll enjoy your company," she added with a hint of amusement in her voice. Now, I do plenty of stuff around the house. I make beds, do dishes, pick dirty socks off the floor, singe food on the grill, mow and fertilize the lawn, take out the garbage and read to the kids. But when my wife said the children would "enjoy my company" she knew I was in for a demanding couple of weeks. In spite of all that I do around the house, giving me full-time, in-control duties like cooking the meals and doing the laundry duty is like placing a weekend jogger in the Boston Marathon. When you are out of shape, it shows.

Which leads me back to sloppy joes. I'd been meaning to scrounge around for that recipe for a few days, but I'd been busy. There was drop off and pick up at summer session. The two younger kids had swimming

6

lessons every day. We staged morning bike rides to the donut shop. I couldn't back out on our plans for a picnic lunch at the park. I had to take the vacuum cleaner in for repairs. And don't forget mountains of dirty laundry.

"Dad! You were supposed to take Mom's sweater out of the dryer. Now it's my size," my eight-year-old daughter scolded me.

"Dad! If we don't leave right now we'll be late for swimming lessons!"

"Dad! The upstairs toilet won't flush!"

And while I struggled to deal with all of this, I'd neglected to locate that sloppy joes recipe, my children's favorite. You can only make macaroni and cheese so many ways before the villagers begin plotting their coup.

I didn't want to call any of my wife's friends for their recipes for fear that they'd label me as incompetent…the only husband in Elk Grove who couldn't toss meat in a pan, dump in ketchup and cook a meal.

"Good Heavens! Haven't you ever heard of Manwich, you idiot!"

So, I turned to the Internet for help. My search for instructions on making slushy beef sandwiches took me off my recipe trail. Actually, I wandered off willingly. Perhaps, I subconsciously was avoiding my date with the frying pan. Somehow, I found a cluster of websites dedicated to what I was doing for such a short time…being a Stay-At-Home Dad. There were chat rooms and support groups and millions of guys apparently needing the available guidance.

According to the Bureau of Labor Statistics, nearly two million American fathers stay at home. The number of fathers ages 24 to 54 who say they have opted not to seek new jobs because of "home responsibilities" jumped from 4.6 percent to 8.4 percent during the 1990s. That's a lot of fathers accepting different responsibilities.

As I sat in front of the computer, subjecting myself to self-analysis over whether I could possibly handle full-time "stay-at-home" duties, my wife walked through the front door after a hard day of teaching. While I fumbled through hundreds of choices for the ultimate sloppy joes preparation process, she plopped the meat in the pan, dropped in ketchup and a few sprinkles of ingredients I couldn't identify and had dinner ready within a few minutes. I felt like a high school basketball player having Kobe Bryant blow past me and make a high-flying slam-dunk.

I learned something by watching. Make things simple. But in order to avoid future shame, I'm going to have a killer sloppy joes recipe hidden and at hand for my own protection.

Another True To Life Cell Phone Survival Story

"I need a new cell phone," my wife groaned. "This one stinks. The battery lasts three calls and the reception is awful."

The cell phone is one of those things that our family has grown dependent upon. Between soccer, basketball, PTA and work how do you coordinate schedules and figure out what to pick up for dinner?

When I was a kid, every house had one phone. It was a black rotary phone with a tangled cord about two feet long. We didn't have call waiting or answering machines. We had busy signals, missed calls and loose change for pay phones. I think the first time I was a "mobile phone" was on "The Man from U.N.C.L.E." Napoleon Solo was zipping around in a red sports car and talking into a phone. To which I thought: "Impossible! It's not connected to the kitchen wall."

I think of cell phones as safety features. When the radiator sizzles and my wife's stranded along some desolate road with a minivan full of soccer players, I want her to be able to get help. She can use her cell phone to either call me at work or call AAA. If she calls me the best mechanical advice I can give her is: "Call AAA!"

So, with our kids staying with friends who live a thirty-minute drive away, my wife and I visited one of our local's cell phone stores in search of a dependable cell phone, one that doesn't sound scratchy like a 1930's radio program and won't crap out while you're in mid-sentence.

The first time we bought a cell phone, we pointed to one at the counter of a department store, took the cheapest service plan and that was it. This time we went to a special "cell phone supplier" and the transaction took more than an hour! We had to sign almost the same amount of paperwork that it took to close on our house.

Did we want the 150 peak minutes plan and the 300 peak minutes plan? What about weekend rates? Call waiting? Digital or analog?

I wanted to say: "My wife just needs a cell phone to call for help if she gets a flat tire! She doesn't need one that has Internet and stock quotes!"

But nothing's simple these days.

"This model offers conference calling," the sales clerk said proudly.

"She doesn't need conference calling unless she and her friends want to play bunco over the phone," I joked.

The unsmiling clerk was unfazed. "Business people like the conference call option."

"How about a basic model, one without the video games and weather radar?"

Once again, the clerk didn't smile. The competition within the cell phone industry must rob the sales people of their sense of humor.

After lengthy deliberation, we chose the model where the people on the box were smiling into their cell phones. They seemed so happy. The model must have been a good one.

An hour later, our hands cramped from the stack of paperwork, my wife had a spiffy maroon cell phone complete with an extra battery, a leather carrying case, a hands-free headset and an owner's manual the size of a Stephen King paperback.

We now also have an extra monthly bill, which means sometimes we'll have to decide between food for the kids or the cell phone.

We left the store for our friend's house to get the kids.

"Call and tell them we're coming," I said.

"Not just yet. I'm busy choosing what type of ring I want," my wife said.

As we drove up Highway-99, my wife treated us to a cell phone symphony. There were—I'm not exaggerating—a thousand sounds from which to choose. There was the National Anthem, Beethoven, Take Me Out to the Ballgame, disco and your basic beep.

"Don't you want to call and tell them we're on our way?" I asked again.

"In a minute," my wife answered. She stared at her phone like a gambler trying to conquer a slot machine.

She chose the funky soul blues ring. She set up her voice mail and pre-programmed several numbers into the speed dial. By the time she was finished playing with the expensive piece of plastic we were parked in front of our friend's house.

"Do you think we need to call ahead now," I asked. "Or can we just go knock on the door?"

LET THE GAMES BEGIN

"What's that in the plastic bag?" I asked my wife. She had just returned from an outing to Wal-Mart, the Mecca of inexpensive household merchandise, the place where you can buy anything from an oil filter to a gallon of milk to underwear before getting your eyes examined by the on-duty optometrist. It was supposed to be a quick trip for a few school supplies. It ended up being a lengthy excursion for a little bit of everything. Among the pencils and notebooks, the paper towels and monster value-packs of candy bars was a little bright red box.

"I bought Yahtzee. From now on we're going to have regular family game nights!" she said.

"That sounds good, but we can't start family game night tonight," I gently protested. "We just picked up *Charlie's Angels* and *Crouching Tiger, Hidden Dragon* at Blockbuster. They're both intellectually intriguing films. And that Cameron Diaz has some great memorable scenes. Can't we have family game night some other night?"

"It's tonight," she said with a definitive tone, pulling the clear plastic off the Yahtzee box like an eager child unwrapping a Christmas present. The highbrow thriller *Charlie's Angels* would have to wait for another night.

We are making an effort—although we are not always successful—at slowing things down in our lives. It isn't easy. The alarm clock goes off early and it's like a starter's pistol. We are off to the races again. Get up, kids. Make your beds. Hurry up! What do you want for breakfast? No, you cannot wear THAT to school! Don't waste time! What's that in your hair? Who's buying lunch today and who's packing? Soccer practice is at 5:30 p.m. The PTA meeting starts at 7:00 p.m. That means dinner at Mickey D's in between. Get home. It's too late to go outside and play. By the way, does anyone have homework to finish? Hey everyone, shower and brush your teeth! Love you. See you in the morning.

The whole day speeds by and yet it seems as if we've spent a total of only fifteen minutes together.

And then the alarm goes off again...

That's pretty much the way of life in a household with two working parents, a house filled with active children and a fast-paced existence that always make you feel as if you are frantically running downhill with no finish line in sight. It's hard to stop when you are gathering that type of furious momentum. Sometimes you have to take a time out. We started with Yahtzee.

We cleared off the dinner table and broke out the dice. We rolled. We cheered. We laughed. We talked about other things besides the game in progress. School. Sports. Friends. The children even trash talked. It sounds different around the dinner table compared to the basketball court. "You got no game, man! You got nothin'." But I ignored their insults and didn't let it distract me. I did the best I could. And as I explained to the children, life is full of ups and downs. We must all try our hardest at whatever we do. We must remember to approach these types of games from a fun point of view. We can't take these games too seriously. It's all in good family amusement and besides the game is basically stupid anyway and someone has to finish in last place and the rest of you cheated any way and I can't believe you kids would treat me that way.

"Family Game Night" is one of those concepts conjured up by the folks from Hasbro and Milton Bradley, the game makers. But it's not like one of those holidays that seem to be invented by the greeting card companies to sell a product. The National Parenting Center had a hand in "Family Game Night" too. Evelyn Peterson is with the National Parenting Center and she believes an occasional family get together to play board games goes a long way toward building stronger bonds.

"What brings families closer and what gives children a sense of belonging is the kind of quality time that happens when family members interact and talk and listen face to face and when they laugh and enjoy each other as people," Peterson once said.

We played Yahtzee for a couple of hours. I guess I'm going to take back what I said about it being a stupid game because someone might misinterpret that as a bitter statement coming from a resentful man who came in last place and was humiliated by the children he loves. However, I am going to work on my game so that I can put those disrespectful, little trash talkers in their places.

In the past, we've gotten together to play cards or others games, but we've never made it a regular thing. We have to try and change that. You can always buy a copy of *Charlie's Angels* and watch it any time but you can't buy quality time spent with your family.

THE IMPORTANCE OF NOTHING

"So who are you chatting with?" I asked my eighth-grade son. He was clicking away at the computer keyboard, involved in a multi-level online conversation with several school friends.

"Just a bunch of the guys," he answered, his fingers flying across the keys. Occasionally my son would laugh when one of his buddies would say—I mean, write—something funny. He was enjoying checking in with his pals.

"You guys trying to get together to play some ball?"

"No. Doesn't look like it. Dan has to go to his grandmother's house. C.J. has something else to do. They're all too busy. We'll play some other time," the intense teen answered, talking and typing at the same time.

No matter how hard they tried it seemed that the guys just could not coordinate a time because of their busy schedules. They had too many things to do. It's something that seems so common these days. A lot of kids have too many things going on; too many things marked down in their daily planners.

I don't know if you have noticed, but it's gotten to the point where kids are having a tough time penciling in "kid time" these days. They always seem to have something on "their schedule" to do. What many of us parents fail to realize is the importance of nothing…as in having nothing to do.

With everything going on, many of today's kids seem kind of stressed. Their parents are DEFINITELY stressed while trying to deal with their own schedules as well as the kid's activities.

We've done it in our house. You've probably done it in yours. We've had soccer, karate lessons, basketball practice, back to school night, religious education classes and homework commitments all competing for time within a short span on the same day. Calendars are jam-packed. Palm Pilots are overloaded with our children's pastimes.

I think it stems from the fact that—at least in my case—we didn't have an over-scheduling problem while I was young because there weren't that many things to schedule. Except for Little League in the summer and the grade school basketball program in the winter, there wasn't much to do when I was growing up. We didn't have swim lessons, indoor soccer, drama and voice classes or martial arts classes available to us. We had pick-up games of tackle football in the vacant lot where we had to avoid slamming someone into a pile of broken glass or a rusty box spring. Bloodletting always resulted in a penalty…and the wrath of someone else's mother. We had that secret spot in the woods—the one everybody knew about—where we staged mud ball battles and fort building. We couldn't get online and e-mail our buddies. We'd either yell out the window or hop on our bikes to see if they could get together. Back then, we had plenty of days with nothing planned and all day to get it done.

When I was a teenager, my buddy Mark owned a 1967 Corvair. His father bought it but Mark was charged with the responsibility of getting the thing running. It was a two-doored, four-wheeled, manual transmissioned nightmare. Mark always had engine parts scattered along the driveway that was decorated with oil and grease stains. Nearly every time I dropped in on Mark, he was either underneath that Corvair yanking out some stubborn engine part or struggling to force some part to fit back inside. I'd talk while he'd work. Within a few minutes we'd both be talking. Within a half-hour we were both in his room listening to his stereo and talking about girls we didn't have the guts to ask out for fear that they would laugh in our faces. Mark and I would find nothing to do and stretch it out over an entire afternoon. After our nothing was done I'd go back home, leaving Mark to clean up his engine fragments before his father clobbered him. I think those times where I had nothing to do are the times I remember the best.

We don't give our kids enough opportunities for doing nothing these days. I think we are trying so hard to make every opportunity available to our children—opportunities that we never had—that we over-book. Sometimes we even feel guilty just kicking back.

As I am writing this at 10:00 Sunday morning, the house is a disaster. It looks like a laundry basket exploded, scattering filthy clothing in all directions. There is a pile of bills screaming to be paid. Two of my children are zoning out to "Sponge Bob Squarepants" cartoons. My middle son is "experimenting" with all the high-pitch sounds that a saxophone can make. My oldest is still in bed, no doubt plotting to pounce on his brother for the unwanted sunrise saxophone serenade. Right now, they're doing nothing and it's fine for a while. We won't let "the nothing" go on all day, but we'll let this down time unravel for a while for four kids and two parents with busy schedules.

Socrates once said: "Not life, but good life, is to be chiefly valued."

I think what old Soc was saying is that sometimes you have to find the time to do nothing and let it linger a long while to appreciate the good life.

RAISING KIDS

"Call them rules or call them limits…they are an expression of loving concern."

Mister Rogers

"The best way to keep children at home is to make the home atmosphere pleasant—and let the air out of their tires."

Dorothy Parker

INTRODUCING THE PRINCESS PROTECTION AGREEMENT

She is only 7 years old, and her idea of a date is a trip to Dairy Queen for a Peanut Buster Parfait with my wife and me. Her notion of a good time is planting flowers in the front yard or baking chocolate chip cookies in the kitchen. She has friends who are boys, but she has no boyfriends. That's the way I like it for my daughter right now. I know all of that is going to change some day when she comes home from school crying because Marcy said that Sandy said that Micki knows that Ashley said that Becky knows what she once said about Rick being cute and how Rick knows that she said what she said but that she didn't want Rick to know and it's all Marcy's fault in the first place and she has no room to talk seeing as how she looks bad in Capri pants.

Do you follow me? If you understand that language, then you know that boys have become, or will soon become, an important part of your little girl's life. I am not ready for that moment. In fact, I'd like to avoid that episode in life as much as anyone would love to cheat death. However, that day will come soon enough and I am trying to brace myself for the inevitable.

Fathers love their sons and fathers love their daughters. But they are two different kinds of love. I know it sounds chauvinistic and condescending to say this but any father will tell you that it's true. In a father's eyes, sons grow up to be men, but daughters grow up and somehow remain little girls.

Dads believe that no matter how old their daughters are that they need protection. Boys also need protection, but they can wait because they are for the most part clueless and content. Boys are fat, dumb and happy gnawing on chicken bones and grunting while watching any sporting event on television. They don't need the same sort of protection as little girls. For fathers, the overwhelming desire to help their sons comes much later in life, like when sons have to be talked out of stupid things like pledging a fraternity, or buying a two-seat foreign sports car with a name you can't even pronounce.

Since I am concentrating on daughter guardianship right now, my advice is to focus on the prospective suitors as the best defense. I don't think it's right to try to simply discourage these guys who become interested in our baby girls. No. It's important to scare the crud out of them! I think it's appropriate to keep prospective suitors in a constant state of panic to the point that they carry around extra underwear in case they run into you.

I am proposing that if any of those mouth breathing, toe jam picking, unworthy slobs are even bold enough to attempt to date our daughters that we allow them to do so under certain restrictive conditions. I am proposing that before they even try to get to know our daughters that we force…excuse me…that we very strongly encourage them to sign the **PRINCESS PROTECTION AGREEMENT**, which reads as follows:

I _____, an admitted blockhead who is clearly unworthy of being in your daughter's presence, do hereby solemnly swear that if I am to date your "PRINCESS", from here on referred to as daughter, that I must meet the following conditions:

I will never look your daughter directly in the eye or talk to her unless she first talks to me and then I may refer to her as "Your Majesty."

I will never try to hold her hand or touch her in any way for fear that I will lose a limb to the chainsaw she wears around her neck.

I will provide your daughter with two-weeks notice if I would like to take her out on a date but understand that she can cancel the date the moment I knock on the front door.

I agree to provide for your review copies of all previous report cards dating back to kindergarten, as well as letters of recommendation from clergyman of three separate faiths and at least one deceased United States President.

I agree that failure to meet these conditions will result in me losing all my rights as a human being no matter what is printed in the U-S Constitution and the Bill of Rights.

Signed,

Sub-Human Boy Whose Name Doesn't Matter

Fathers please keep several copies of this agreement in your car at all times as well as posted on your front door. Daughters, you may think these guidelines are terribly unfair, but in the words of that famous philosopher Socrates, who tried desperately to keep all those Greek guys and their floppy togas away from his baby girl—too bad!

I love my daughter and want the best for her, but when the time comes for her to start dating, those poor unsuspecting saps that call will have to read and memorize the "PRINCESS PROTECTION AGREEMENT." As they commit this agreement to memory, they also should remember, most importantly, that if they ever do go out, they should have a really good time.

If my daughter tells me she didn't have a good time I'll let you know.

REAL LIFE CAUGHT ON TAPE

We must be a Stone Age family by today's standards. We don't have cable television, or a satellite dish, or a DVD player. We don't use Palm Pilots to electronically log our important dates and events. The dog-eared calendar stuck to the refrigerator with magnets, and covered with scribbling in pen, pencil and crayon does the trick for us. What makes our family seem freakish to many people is the fact that we do not own something almost as common as a VCR or a George Foreman cooker. We do not own a video camera.

For some people, that makes us simply Jurassic.

I'd like to own a videocam. And we've been meaning to get one. It's just that it's an expensive item and usually we need to spend our money on other things like the mortgage or food maybe.

It would be great to have videos of all the kid's school plays, basketball games and birthday parties, but snapshots have to do for now. We'll eventually get around to buying a video camera some day like when the grandchildren learn to walk, but for now, if I really want moving pictures of my children all I need to do is check with the managers of some of our favorite stores and restaurants in the area. I know it seems kind of weird, but if those managers were to carefully scan their surveillance tapes, they'd see my kids in action.

I'm not talking about burglary action, or shoplifting. We routinely check their pockets before we leave stores, just as a precaution. It became a habit because when the children were much, much younger we left a few stores with an occasional candy bar that somehow mysteriously slipped into a coat pocket.

The type of action I'm talking about involves real live, full blown, honest to Pete performances! Whenever my four children are together in a store, and see a surveillance camera pointed in their direction it is LIGHTS, CAMERA, and ACTION! The hams see a lense pointed their way and a variety show spontaneously breaks out. They'll make faces. They'll dance. They'll do anything goofy if they know a video camera is aimed at them.

The kids do have their favorite performance venues. They like the Carl's Jr. about a mile from our house the best. That one has a crystal clear color television screen to accompany the camera and it's in full view of everyone standing at the counter. And, of course, the better the picture, the better the performance. Their shows are short, just long enough to place an order at the cash register and grab a stack of drink cups. But it's amazing that in that short amount of time, a group of four kids can stage an impromptu performance of Tony Award quality…if only the Carl's Jr. was located on Broadway (the one in New York) and not just off Highway-99 in Elk Grove, California.

When we go into any store, in addition to checking out the merchandise, my kids look over the surveillance equipment. They aren't casing the stores or planning any criminal activities. They're just looking at camera angles and lighting. If the cameras are well hidden, my cast of characters cancel the show and wait for the next opportunity to perform. But if the cameras are in plain view, then it could be an N*SYNC dance number, or maybe a reenacted scene from *The Matrix*.

I have to wonder if the security guys, squeezed into some back storage room are enjoying the productions my kids put on, or is this something common among bored children standing in line while their parents order cheeseburgers with bacon or search for 100-percent cotton shirts? Maybe we can get ten-percent off our next purchase at Staples if the kids can form the human pyramid without knocking over that display of gel pens near the cash register.

When I was a kid, my Uncle Ray had the coolest home movie camera. It was as big as a cinder block with a rack of lights perched on top that were bright enough to land planes.

"Just be yourselves!" Uncle Ray would shout as he blinded us with his movie lights. "Just act naturally!" And that, of course, was our cue to behave like circus freaks which we did whenever possible.

We haven't yet found an local store that has a rack of blinding lights, but if and when we do, I'm sure you'll find my kids there...just acting naturally.

DEALING WITH THE BIG ANXIETY OF GOING TO A BIGGER SCHOOL

The only real constant in life is change. I forget who coined that famous phrase, but it certainly applies to a lot of things. However, I'm confident whoever uttered that truism was either a scholarly observer of the world…or more than likely someone who had a kid going into junior high.

I can see the scenario. There's a parent whose child was facing the prospects of leaving the safety of elementary school and entering into seventh grade with great apprehension. The child obviously needed the kind of guidance that only an insightful mother or father can provide. So, the parent reached deep down into a personal pool of wisdom to offer comfort and enlightenment.

"Well, I know you might be a little scared about things being different next year, but remember: The only real constant in life is change!"

To which the nervous child presumably replied: "What does that have to do with rushing to different rooms between class periods, dealing with school dances, or sharing a huge cafeteria with 1,500 other kids? And in gym class, are they going to make me climb that stupid rope up to the gymnasium ceiling?"

Those are fair questions.

My oldest son is bracing himself for next year's transition from sixth grade to seventh grade. While he is not consumed with anxiety—like his mother and I—he *is* experiencing some uneasiness.

Going from elementary school, with recesses, staying in the same classroom for most of the day and sharing that classroom with kids they've known since kindergarten, to a bigger, unfamiliar campus, with no recesses and being surrounded by strange kids from several different schools who threaten to hold you up by your ankles and take your lunch money, is a big deal. And while the child is dealing with those anxieties, we parents have a locker full of our own concerns: drugs, alcohol, more drugs, sex and gangs. The older a child gets, the more influential friends become and the more intense the peer pressure. It gets harder every year.

Junior high is a big transition. It's a big step up the ladder into that strange area where a kid is still a kid but certainly no longer a child. There's a lot of anxiety during this time, for the parents and their offspring.

As he heads into junior high, my oldest has a laundry list of concerns. (We won't call them worries.) Will he have classes with other kids he knows? Will he be able to find his way around the campus? Will the older kids at his new school be looking to pick on the younger ones? Will the homework be too much to handle?

Last week, we were going over all these questions as we sat at a corner table at Original Mel's. We munched on burgers, slurped milk shakes and talked about our anxiety associated with going to a new school, about making new friends and starting over. Our younger children were not lending anything to the conversation, other than complaining about who was stealing fries and who was using too much ketchup. (Like there's a limit!) Then, someone did contribute to our conversation. He was a young man who works at Mel's. He was cleaning the table next to ours.

"I'm sorry for interrupting," the young man said. "But I overheard your conversation." Then he looked at my son, tossed a dishtowel over his shoulder and said: "I've moved around a lot. I used to live in Kentucky, then I moved back and now I am going to the high school. I have to tell you that once you go to another school, you're really not friends with the same kids from elementary school. And it's easier to make new friends than you think. I've done it." Then he apologized again for interrupting. We thanked him for his advice, and he went back to work.

I'm sorry I didn't get the young man's name. He seemed like an intuitive and compassionate guy willing to help a younger kid through an anxious situation. It was good for our son to hear from someone other than his parents that things are going to be okay.

I'm sure if the young man had told my son that the only real constant in life is change that my son would have understood.

THE SHIRT OFF MY BACK

"That shirt isn't mine."

My wife looked confused. There's no way she was wrong. She's a pro in the laundry separation department.

"Look at it. Are you sure?" my wife asked. I could tell that she didn't appreciate me questioning her clothing expertise. That would be like asking Martha Stewart if she really understood where to place the salad forks on the dinner table.

The t-shirts, sweat socks and underwear were systematically folded and separated on the bed like they had been a million times before. As always, the shirts go on the bottom of the pile. The undies go on top of the shirts, followed by the socks on the very peak of the mound. It had been a flawless practice since the kids were born. Now the method doesn't work as well and we blame our two oldest sons.

They are seventh and eighth graders and are growing so rapidly that we can almost hear their bodies stretching. The result—along with meteoric food bills—is the creation of a massive clothing confusion in our home.

Sometimes it's not hard to tell some of my clothing from theirs, with simple things like socks and shorts. My underwear is bigger and has more holes, but it's only a matter of time before the boys catch up to me in the undergarment department. Eventually, I'll reach the point when I cannot find a perfectly broken in pair of Hanes, that I'll no longer be able to blame my wife for tossing them in the trash. I'll have to go looking in my son's drawers for my drawers.

The good news for me is that I'm in that "comfortable fit" stage of my life where the more stretchy the elastic in the waistband the better I feel. If you pull the elastic band and it doesn't snap back, chance are those are my undies.

A few weeks ago, I couldn't find my tennis shoes. I looked in the closet, under the bed and even in the trunk of my car. That last place I thought to look was the last place I looked...on the feet of my seventh grader.

"Hey, gimme those. That's the only pair I have that doesn't have grass stains from mowing the lawn."

"They fit me pretty good," my size eight shoe-wearing son said proudly. "My feet are only a half size smaller than yours."

All at once, I felt old.

I wasn't expecting this to happen for years. Sure, I planned on losing t-shirts here and there. But I didn't think I'd start losing apparel to my kids until they were well into their teenage years and wanted to dress up for costume parties to go as a dorky parent.

My dress shirts and ties are safe. At least, for now. But I know it's only a matter of time before they start disappearing.

The only apparel defense I really have right now is this: never own any clothes that they'd really be interested in taking. One would have to figure that no pre-teen or teenage son in his right mind would be caught dead wearing anything that his father purchased at Target, Sears or Ross. Those are all fine stores, but no young gentleman interested in looking his coolest could bear to have clothing from those stores touch their skin.

"Hey, son. Would you like to borrow this nifty white button down dress shirt that I got for half price at Men's Warehouse?"

"No thanks. I think I'll just dig around in the clothes hamper and scrape the mud off something wrinkled."

Actually, I am looking forward to turning the clothing tables on them some day.

When the boys are bigger than I am (which at this rate could be by next Christmas) I will take every opportunity to rifle through their dressers looking for clothes. What I like, I'll wear. What I don't like lands on the floor. That's the way they do it.

And some day it'll come to a head when I hear one of my sons yell:

"What happened to all of my blue Nike t-shirts? DAD!!!!"
It will be a happy day indeed.

Sometimes A Girl Has Just Got To Twirl

She posed before us, looking splendid in her magnificent white dress. Her face shined brighter than the whiter-than-white shoes tightly strapped to her fidgety feet. The sheer, milky veil perched atop her head of meticulously curled hair flowed with every move she made.

And the girl could not help but twirl. After all, it was her First Communion Day. Twirling was her God given right.

In the Catholic Church, making your First Communion is a monumental step. It gives children a greater connection to their faith. It also provides little girls with the opportunity to dress like brides and endure all the punishment that three older brothers can deliver.

When a little girl makes her First Communion only a select few words can suitably describe her that day: beautiful, radiant, picturesque. Or in the words of her older brothers: annoying or irritating.

"Dad! She's twirling again!"

One of her brothers was trying to watch some significant cartoon show, but his view was obstructed by the flowing white dress of a little sister. Every step she took was a confident stride. Every turn she made was a willowy pirouette. She was wearing a beautiful white dress and a veil and when an eight-year-old girl wears something that special, she just has to twirl.

The magnificent outfit altered her behavior. It transformed her from a lanky little girl who trips over her own feet into an agile and flowing ballerina. Each step she took had a purpose. Every movement had meaning. Each and every twirl was a statement.

She would spin much too closely to one of the boys clutching a Nintendo controller and we'd hear: "Make her stop!"

Even a little sister dressed like a princess on her First Communion Day has no right to interfere with a possible all-time high *Mario Brothers* score.

"Don't mind her," my wife and I would say. "She's just twirling. It'll pass."

As we walked out of the house to make our way to church, our daughter promenaded. As we climbed into the minivan, one member of the entourage ascended. We drove in the midst of a small amount of traffic, which at least one of us may have imagined to be a full-blown parade.

One of the boys tugged at baby sister's veil and she went from lamb to lioness. "Quit it!" she shrieked. "You'll mess it up!" My wife and I tried to hold back our smiles.

"Make her take off the veil," one of the boys laughed. "It's making her act different."

When we arrived at Good Shepherd Church, we found a flock of handsome little boys decked out in jackets and ties, and gorgeous little girls festooned in fancy white dresses, just right for sauntering.

"Honey, try to hold off on your twirling for a while," we advised our daughter. We feared she'd knock over some burning candles or fall into the baptismal font. And since she was not alone, since she was sharing this day with a bunch of eight-year-old girls doodled up in flowing white dresses in one room, it increased the chances of careless twirling accidents. Little boys, in their neckties and dress shirts look handsome, but you know they're still ready for a wrestling match at a moment's notice. Little girls, in fine formal attire, are poised for portraits but reckless twirling in a crowd could cause some serious Communion Day catastrophes.

The mass began and the children paraded in. We were relieved to see our daughter walking solemnly, not spinning. When it came time for her to receive Communion, she smiled broadly as she approached the altar.

"Oh, no," I whispered to my wife. "I think she's going to twirl."

Fortunately, she didn't. She controlled herself and received communion without any unnecessary dance movements.

Finally, after mass, it was time for photos. I took several pictures of my daughter with Father Philip Wells, our pastor, and some of the other kids in her class. And with a few pictures left on the roll, we placed our tiny dancer near the altar and said "TWIRL!"

She did. She twirled and pirouetted and her fancy white dress lifted slightly as she spun. We still haven't developed the film, so we're not sure if last few snapshots came out. Even if they don't, I'll always have that mental picture of a blissful, spinning little girl etched in my mind.

EDUCATION

"You are educated when you have the ability to listen to almost anything without losing your temper or self-confidence."

Robert Frost

"Time is a great teacher, but unfortunately it kills all its pupils."

Hector Louis Berlioz (1803-1869) French Composer

Warthogs And William

"It would be a positive relief to dig him up and throw stones at him."

(George Bernard Shaw referring to
Shakespeare)

Maybe George Bernard Shaw was having a bad day when he launched such a nasty insult in the direction of William Shakespeare who, at the time of that comment, was considered one of the greatest insult artists in history and also very dead and unable to properly defend himself.

Had Shakespeare been around to hear Shaw's criticism, he might have countered with a stinging remark like: "Thou craven fly-bitten minnow!" Back in Shakespeare's day that was probably a step short of saying something derogatory about someone's mother.

Many of the past great leaders in the world of literature were not fans of Shakespeare. The same probably goes for your average person today, including most professional athletes (I'm guessing here), the majority of people who have season tickets to monster truck shows and middle-aged balding guys who write local newspaper columns.

I've never been a Shakespeare fan and never will be. In high school, we read and dissected both *Hamlet* and *Macbeth* in one semester. Frankly, I don't remember much about either play. I remember that people died. Most of the characters didn't seem like very nice people. There were witches and ghosts, which gave the dead people something to do rather than just lie there. Overall, I found Shakespeare's work very confusing.

However, I am gaining a new appreciation for Will's work and I have my oldest son to thank. He's a seventh grade student and has studied

Shakespeare in literature classes. I was certain that he'd zone out while studying works like *The Tempest,* but he's become a fan of the English playwright and poet who died in 1616. He's not a Shakespeare admirer because of the artist's use of verse to express the deepest levels of human motivation. My son enjoys Shakespeare because the old guy was good with the insult.

My son recently went on a field trip to Ashland, Oregon for the big Shakespeare festival that's always held there. He came back with a new appreciation for the creator of such classics as *Much Ado About Nothing* and *Romeo and Juliet,* not for the frilly prose but for the cool way Shakespeare could slight people with such interesting and hard to understand words.

He also returned from his trip with a book on Shakespeare, but it wasn't about the dramatist's flowery phrasing as much it was about his acidic insults. Now when my son and his friends want to verbally abuse each other with a sense of style they don't blurt out words like dork, geek, loser or anything of the socially unacceptable variety. Instead, they take their time and flip through their trusty Shakespeare insult guide to find gems like:

"Thou spleeny earth-vexing hedge-pig!"

"Thou impertinent ill-breeding miscreant!"

"Your face is not worth sunburning!"

And of course, "You have such a February face, so full of frost, of storm and cloudiness."

The great thing about quoting Shakespeare while insulting someone is that it seems like a high brow way to zing a person when you're using words that might not even be understood if there was a dictionary handy.

For example, if I was just pulling into an open parking space at Raley's and some jerk, who knew I was waiting for THAT space, cut in front of me with his dented 1976 AMC Pacer, I could get out of my car and matter-of-factly say: "Thou weedy boil-brained warthog!" Then, I could go in, get my gallon of milk and leave before he's finished scratching his head in confusion.

It may not be the best way to go about it, but maybe by studying Shakespeare's insults and barbs, kids like my son and his classmates can gain an appreciation for the legendary writer's mastery of the English language.

If you don't agree, then maybe you should be considered a "full-gorged malt worm" or a "hasty-witted scut."

I'm not sure what those words mean. I'll have to ask my son.

THE ART OF PROCRASTINATION: A FAMILY PROJECT

It seemed like a perfect Sunday morning, that slow and easy time to curl up on the couch with a cup of coffee and the newspaper and actually spend time reading it. The sky was gray and the ground was damp from one steady rain that had another threatening to follow. It was the perfect time…to panic.

Time was running out. It wasn't possible to enjoy any of life's little pleasures because of that dark cloud hanging overhead…the dreaded homework project cloud.

That's what happens when your kids have science projects due in a few days and you are fairly certain that the bulk of the work didn't get done way ahead of time.

When a child has a science project due, that usually means the parents also have a science project due. It is an involuntary group effort. It's not a complaint because some projects are fun, but it's a fact that these things develop into family projects.

The first step involves procrastination. Your child knows the project deadline is looming even though it is weeks and weeks away. Everyone tosses around ideas, but no one settles on anything concrete. The project gets put on the back burner because…well…there's other homework…and soccer or basketball…followed by church…toss in a sleep-over or two…not to mention watching "Survivor", the bug-eating episode on tape that you've been meaning to watch again. The next thing you know, the science fair is swiftly closing in and you know there's some obnoxious, know-it-all kid who's going to clone a sheep or create nuclear fusion using common kitchen cleaners and you don't want your own child to look foolish.

Angst. Desperation. Fear. These are emotions that you are experiencing because your kid knows you will help him pull through. You always do.

About a week before the assignment is due you storm Borders where a brief conversation with a bookstore clerk goes like this:

YOU: Do you have a book on fast and easy, last minute, down to the wire elementary school science projects that can be done without a hundred yards of chicken wire or a bucket of moldy bread?

CLERK: We just sold the last one. But we do have one remaining copy of *Duplicating the Life of a Giant Sequoia Tree One-Year at a Time.*

Before you know it, the deadline is only days away. Panicked, you hop in the car, not remembering if you've brushed your teeth, and you drive to the nearest store for project supplies. You reach Staples and realize the place doesn't open until 10am on Sundays. You cruise past the local craft store, and it doesn't open for another hour either. (Shouldn't stores have extended weekend hours when elementary school students have science projects due?) Next, you try Target, which gets points for being open, but also loses points for not having what you need. Then, you drive to Office Depot and that place doesn't open for another fifteen minutes. So, you waste time collecting all the candy wrappers, church bulletins, hair clips and empty juice boxes that have accumulated inside the car. Eventually, the manager unlocks the front door and you race inside to buy the last remaining Scholar Pro Display Board ™ without knocking over any parents competing for the same science project supplies.

Finally, you return home where there's a mysterious calmness. Everyone asks what all the fuss was about. It turns out that the kids have pecked away at the science project over time, doing a little bit here and there. They've already completed their research. They have the pictures they need and just have to put everything together. They're just waiting on you and the Scholar Pro Display Board ™ you were supposed to buy days ago.

Funny but it seems that it's you and not the kids putting off every last blessed thing until the last blessed minute. Somehow it all gets done.

"How about next year we do a science project on procrastination and its impact on a parent's stress level?" you ask with a frail laugh in your voice. They all glare at you, then turn away and focus on their work again.

Next year, I'm in charge of the poster board. Unless you want to get it.

AND NOW FOR SOMETHING COMPLETELY DIFFERENT

Sometimes different generations don't "click". There's a barrier blocking them. Finding common ground is difficult.

In our house, we've tried music as a "Gap Bridger" but it's never worked. The music I like makes the boys cover their ears. My sons like music that makes me want to cover their ears so they can't hear the lyrics. Anything that's not accompanied by a music video on MTV performed by an all male or all female group wearing bizarre costumes is considered an oldie.

Some day I'll introduce them to KISS. Anyway…

Sports worked for a while, but I can't keep up any more. My boys are 13, 11 and almost 10. They always beat me to the hoop when we're playing basketball. They out run and out rebound me. They don't out-sweat me, but eventually, they taunt me, and then I leave to rest my aching knees. It's a vicious cycle.

But I've found something that bridges that gap of misunderstanding between my sons and me and it's something that I want all you fathers out there to consider using…

Monty Python!

Yes, that off the wall English comedy troupe helped create a better cultural understanding between my sons and me.

A few weeks ago, the boys were enjoying a television program with a hint of English humor and it gave me an idea.

"If you like this, you're probably ready for Monty Python," I said, baiting them.

"What's that? Some kind of snake?", one of the boys chuckled.

I explained what Monty Python was all about, and how we thought the show was the funniest thing on TV way back in the Jurassic 70's. My sales pitch was failing until I offered this clincher: "You'll like them. They're really stupid!"

SOLD! Anything stupid is okay with them. Anything really stupid is essential. So, the next day my wife took the boys to Blockbuster Video and they rented the highly idiotic "Monty Python and the Holy Grail". It's a 1974 film tracing the not-so-suave King Arthur and his hapless Knights of the Round Table in search of the Holy Grail.

Before watching the movie, I reminded them of the tale of King Arthur and the Knights of the Round Table and that it had nothing to do with pizza. Then, I explained that English humor can be absurd, foolish and childish, like Jim Carrey with an accent. After my brief tutorial on the finer points of British humor, we were ready to make our cerebral connection stronger.

In short, the boys loved the film, every last absurd bit of it. They laughed, and then hit the rewind button, laughed some more and hit rewind again. They have now adopted lines from the movie as part of their common language.

When one of them gets slightly hurt, they'll say in a British accent: "It's just a flesh wound."

(In the film, that's what the Black Knight says after Arthur slices off one of the Knight's arms. It's funny, really. No, I'm serious. It is.)

When two of the boys are wrestling and one is hopelessly pinned, the one with no chance of winning says with an English tone: "All right, we'll call it a draw."

(In the movie, that's what the Black Knight says after the king has severed the Knight's every limb and the gallant challenger is too proud to accept defeat. Trust me, it's hilarious!)

At last, after so many attempts through the wholesome approach, we made an intellectual (and I use that word loosely) connection. We had finally come to a cognitive understanding, and it felt good.

With this comedy camaraderie gushing throughout the house, we tried to enlist my wife into our troupe of Monty Python fans. It wasn't going to be easy. Moms are on a "different cognitive plane" when it comes to humor. Moms just don't understand the intricacies of The Three Stooges, or The Pink Panther, or other forms of comedy that don't require much brain activity to enjoy. Monty Python was going to be a hard sell. After some badgering, my wife agreed to sit in front of the TV and watch a group of simpletons search for the Holy Grail. We watched her as she watched this classic comedy. A few smiles peeked through, followed by some eye rolling, followed by that "I don't get it" look. Finally, she laughed. We had a miracle breakthrough. She actually laughed several times (when she wasn't dozing) but would not admit she actually "liked" the movie. However it was a first step for her, a big step for family comedy unity.

Unfortunately, Mom made the mistake of seeking reciprocation.

"Okay, now you boys can sit with me and watch YOU'VE GOT MAIL! with Tom Hanks and Meg Ryan…"

My wife popped the tape in the VCR and her sons fled screaming. Moe, Larry and Curly banged into each other and couldn't leave the room fast enough. Their exit would have made Peter Sellers envious.

There is such a thing as too much intellectual stimulation for one day.

"All right, we'll call it a draw!" as the Black Knight would say.

THE HOME IS ALIVE (?) WITH THE SOUND OF MUSIC (?)

When you have four kids, your house tends to get a little loud. Actually, that's an understatement. When you have four kids, your house tends to sound like *Saving Private Ryan,* only without the weaponry and with a lot less bloodshed.

The arguing and fighting among the kids can be fierce. It gets to be like the *Jenny Jones Show,* only our kids don't talk with twangs, they are not disrespectful and we don't have to bleep out any of their words.

There are times when I wonder whether our neighbors have either gotten used to us or have soundproofed their own homes. Living next to us is not like living near a crowded football stadium on a Friday night, but it's close.

This is why we try to reduce the noise level within our home whenever we can. We keep the television volume at a level safe enough to keep the picture tube from cracking. When the windows start rattling, we crank the CD player down a few notches. (Does homeowner's insurance cover the costs of a window broken by the sounds of Will Smith or N*SYNC?)

In our quest for quietude, my wife and I make an effort to keep noisy things out of our house. We don't allow whistles, noisemakers, or anything so earsplitting that it will rattle your teeth. But now we are welcoming some new sounds. They are strange sounds. Curious sounds for sure. One of my kids has decided he wants to learn a musical instrument.

"Mom, they're having a meeting at school about music classes!" my 6th grade son said one day. "I want to learn to play something!"

His announcement was kind of surprising since we're not a very musical family. My wife had some piano and voice lessons when she was younger. Personally, I can't carry a tune in a bucket. Combine those two facts and the chances of having a musical prodigy for a child becomes extremely slim.

I balked slightly at first because a musical instrument equals loss of quietude. That was a threat to our quest. If we were thinking of putting a musical instrument—any kind of musical instrument—in the hands of a beginner we might as well have said, "Here, son, why don't you strangle this cat for a while every day for at least an hour at a time?"

But on the other hand, learning a musical instrument would be a good experience. Plus anything to keep him off the blasted razor scooter or skateboard to reduce the risk of injury is fine by me. I don't think learning a musical instrument can be physically risky, unless you pick the bagpipes, and flirt with getting stomped by people who hate that "fingernails on a blackboard" kind of music.

"What instrument do you want to learn?" my wife asked.

"I don't know. Maybe the drums."

Great! There's nothing better to raise the decibel level in any home than to add a drum set to a kid's bedroom decor. But then again, if the drumming gets too annoying, we can always crank up the stereo. And when the neighbors bang on the door to complain or ring the doorbell, who is going to hear them any way?

So my wife took our middle son to the school meeting and one the first things the teacher said was…Be warned now. We can't have fifty kids playing the drums!

Time to pick another—hopefully more quiet, less stress inducing—instrument.

"How about the saxophone?" my wife whispered. My son squinted his eyes, unsure about that suggestion. Saxophones are loud, but are probably harder to learn than the drums. And a saxophone does make a really high pitched squeal that only dogs can hear.

Then my wife said, "You know the girls dig sax players."

Sold! My son laughed and nodded in agreement. The next thing I know, we're renting a saxophone and my son is chomping at the bit to be the next David Sanborn. He's only had the instrument for about a week. He can't play anything on it yet, but he's gotten really good at getting the sax out of its case, putting it together and placing the strap around his neck. It's good that he's getting that skill down. You never know when you'll need split second timing to assemble your saxophone and knock out a song at a moment's notice.

To be truthful, he's really excited about learning the sax. His passion for learning music might fade as quickly as some of his other interests have faded, but kids have to try different activities to see what they like. He may never be another Charlie Parker, but he can have fun trying.

David Sanborn once said: "When you're playing with people and you connect, that moment is worth everything you had to go through to get there."

And while my son is trying to connect with those moments, we'll try to keep the noise down.

THERE IS NO GOOD EXCUSE FOR BAD EXCUSES

It's not easy when your child is sick and has to miss school. If there are two working parents in the house, it usually means one of you has to stay home, dig out the extra blankets, brew some hot chocolate and watch the same Arthur and Mary Kate and Ashley videos that you've seen a million times over.

If some ambitious cable television company wanted to make some real money, they would launch "The Sick Kids Network." Kids staying at home with the sniffles, the flu or the dreaded "I didn't finish that homework project" bug would be glued to that channel for hours on end. Advertisers offering vitamins, cold remedies and school supplies would pump millions of dollars worth of advertising into this channel.

Now, when you're dealing with a sick child, one of the first things you have to do is call the school and tell someone in the attendance office that your kid won't be in that day and why. While a majority of the reasons for absences are legitimate, a handful of them really sound sort of fishy. Actually, they stink out loud. On one occasion I volunteered in the office at Barbara Comstock Morse, where my elementary school kids attend. It was the beginning of the school day and some of the students coming in and asking for late slips offered entertaining reasons why they were tardy.

"Why were you late, son?", I asked one little boy.

"We were watching TV," he answered casually.

"Young lady, why are you late?" I asked. "I had to go back and brush my teeth," she answered.

And two of my personal favorite excuses were "I stepped on a bug" and "I couldn't find the right pants."

My wife teaches kindergarten part-time and once, a mother brought her child in late for school and apologized saying "I slept in." The odd thing was that her child attended the **afternoon** kindergarten session that began at around noon. Go figure.

Sometimes parents write notes explaining a child's absence from school. The following are some excuses that friends have sent me from what we should call "the most outlandish excuses" collection. These are actual school absence notes. I'm not sure if any of them, or how many of them, have circulated throughout our school district or yours, but these are excuse notes from parents (including original spelling) collected by schools from all over the country.

Warning to parents: please don't use the following lame excuses as some kind of a study guide for future note writing!

- My son is under a doctor's care and should not take P.E. today. Please execute him.
- Please excuse Lisa for being absent. She was sick and I had her shot.
- Dear School: Please ekscuse John being absent on Jan. 28, 29, 30, 31,32, and also 33.
- Please excuse Roland from P.E. for a few days. Yesterday he fell out of a tree and misplaced his hip.
- John has been absent because he had two teeth taken out of his face.
- Chris will not be in school cus he has an acre in his side.
- Please excuse Ray Friday from school. He has very loose vowels.
- Please excuse Pedro from being absent yesterday. He had [diahre] [dyrea] [direathe]…he had the (inappropriate word inserted here.) [*The words in brackets were crossed out.*]
- Please excuse Jimmy for being. It was his father's fault.
- I kept Billie home because she had to go Christmas shopping because I don't know what size she wear.

- Please excuse Jennifer for missing school yesterday. We forgot to get the Sunday paper off the porch, and when we found it Monday, we thought it was Sunday.
- Sally won't be in school a week from Friday. We have to attend her funeral.
- My daughter was absent yesterday because she was tired. She spent a weekend with the Marines.
- Please excuse Jason for being absent yesterday. He had a cold and could not breed well.

If you are a teacher, I hope you have never been on the receiving end of some of these comical excuses. If you have, I hope that you've remembered to share with others for a good laugh.

One lesson that I think is obvious from this is that the parents who were the authors of these weak and lame notes should consider spending more time in school themselves to work on their writing skills.

Planning For Future Education Without Any Plans

It seemed like a harmless school project, one designed to get the kids thinking about higher education. Instead, the whole thing got me thinking about money, and about how we're going to need truckloads of it in the not too distant future.

My oldest son is a sixth grader. He came home from school last week with an interesting homework project. The assignment was to pick a few colleges that interested them, research and dig up everything they can about those schools and then contact them for admissions material for a class report.

"That sounds like a harmless and fun project," I said to my wife when she told me about the choose-a-college homework. "What schools did he pick?"

"He it narrowed it down to Stanford and Yale," my wife said, with amazement mixed with sadness in her voice. She was acting as if those institutions of higher learning really were his choices and we had to start rummaging through the cabinets for spare drinking glasses and used and battered cookware for him to stuff in the back of the car for his long trip to campus.

"Stanford and Yale?", I answered with fatherly pride. "He has some high goals, doesn't he?"

However, after a few minutes basking in the glow of a daydream about my oldest child attending one of the finest universities in the country, graduating at the top of his class and then accepting a grotesquely high paying job that would allow him to buy his loving parents anything they desired like a nice house in Tahoe, the reality hit me like a ton of bricks. Better make that a ton of GOLD bricks.

"Stanford and Yale are grotesquely expensive schools!" I told my wife. All she could do was nod in stunned agreement.

That started to get me thinking about college…about the parties and the late nights…and the football games…and that one girl, I forget her name but she had…then I stopped and realized I should be thinking about HIS college days and not mine.

I did some research and discovered that unless we hit the Lotto or come into an unexpected pile of money from a wealthy relative we never knew about, that paying for Stanford or Yale will make things pretty tight around the Herrera household. It'll be grilled cheese sandwiches and potato chips forever…and that includes Thanksgiving and Christmas dinners.

As of this writing, if you want to attend the beautiful Palo Alto campus of Stanford, be prepared to shell out a lot of cash. Stanford's tuition is a healthy $22,100 a year. And that does not include room and board, books and other related living expenses like a freezer full of fish sticks and tater tots.

Interested in Yale, are you? New Haven, Connecticut is gorgeous, especially in the fall when the leaves are turning. And about the only thing you'll be able to afford to do there for amusement is watching the leaves turn, because the annual tuition at Yale is a vein bursting $29,950!

Then I made the huge mistake of doing the math. Let's see, if Yale costs around $30,000 a year, multiply that by four years, add in room and board, living expenses, etc…and that comes out to about a gazillion dollars. Or at least it might as well be a gazillion.

When I was on the Internet, I found one of those college calculator websites, but I didn't even bother to calculate. The first line on the site read: "If you're starting 10 to 18 years before college, congratulations! You're way ahead of the game!"

Well, guess what? College for my oldest after this semester is only six years away. That means I'm way behind and not ahead of the game!

It also means, we've got a lot of work ahead of us. In our house, we'll have college tuition times four children. We're going to be encouraging them to work hard for those sports and academic scholarships. We're going to be applying for every grant under the sun. We also might buy an occasional lottery ticket.

I don't know whether the point of the choose-a-college project was to get the young sixth graders to start thinking about their futures, or to get their parents to buckle down and really start planning for the inevitable financial burden of attending an institution of higher learning. Either way, it worked.

SPORTS

"Sports are positively essential. It is healthy to engage in sports, they are beautiful and liberal, liberal in the sense that nothing serves quite as well to integrate social classes, etc., than street or public games."

Anton Chekhov (1860-1904), Russian
author, playwright

"Sports is the toy department of human life."

Howard Cosell

How A Pro Athlete Made A Kid Feel Like A King

Sometimes a small gesture can mean a great deal to a child. And it's nice to cross paths with someone who recognizes the impact they can have on kids.

Peja Stojakovic is a six-foot nine-inch forward for the Sacramento Kings. He's from Serbia and he's one of the NBA's emerging stars. And my youngest son will forever remember Peja as the pro ballplayer who took a few seconds to give some kids a thrill.

My youngest boy's tenth birthday was approaching and he had one request he kept repeating over and over.

"Can we go to a Kings game for my birthday?"

You need to understand that the boy is a Kings fanatic. His room is plastered with Kings posters. If a Kings game is televised, my son is glued to the set. If the game's on the radio, he's in his room, banging into the furniture while shooting hoops on his miniature basket. If the Kings win, he's ecstatic. If they lose, he's bummed.

The Maloof family may own the franchise but the Kings are HIS team.

Because Kings tickets are in great demand, I had to go through a broker to get tickets. Brokers are guys who buy event tickets at regular prices and re-sell them at enormously high prices to people like desperate fathers eager to fulfill birthday wishes. It's safe to say no one else in Section 222 at Arco Arena paid as much to see the Kings play the Dallas Mavericks a few Sundays ago.

My son wanted to go to Arco early to get autographs from some of the players. I told him not to get his hopes up, but when we reached the arena, Kings Darrick Martin, Jabari Smith and Art Long remained on the court working out. These were guys who spent more time watching the game from the bench that season rather than actually playing the game. We stood on the sidelines, surrounded by kids, dressed like my son in a Kings uniform, hoping for autographs. The players graciously obliged, scribbling their names on T-shirts, programs and posters.

"It's great that you got some autographs for your birthday!" I told my son, who was having a blast.

Then an hour before tip-off, Stojakovic came out for extra warm-ups. He stood on the perimeter of the basket, launching long distance shots. Watching Peja Stojakovic shoot a basketball is like watching Mark McGwire swing a baseball bat. For a sports fan, it's a thing of beauty.

Eventually, the Serbian star was just a few feet in front of us when IT happened.

Peja quickly turned to face the throng of young fans and tossed the ball toward the crowd. My son's eyes grew wide as the ball bounced closer. His hands shook. No doubt his ten years of life flashed before his eyes. Good heavens, Peja was passing him the ball! Here was one of the greatest shooters in the game tossing him the ball. It bounced between my son and another boy also dressed in a full Kings uniform. Both stunned boys fumbled with the ball, and then my son grabbed it and instinctively flipped it back to Stojakovic. Peja snatched the ball, turned toward the hoop and swished another jumper.

The small crowd cheered. My son was speechless. I was overwhelmed.

This pro basketball player, a man my boy idolizes, took a few seconds for a quick game of catch.

Fans standing in the small crowd commented on my son's big moment.

"Dude, do you know Peja?"

"Nice pass buddy!"

"That's your first NBA assist, pal!"

"What a great birthday present," I said.

Maybe that ball was intended for the crowd, but my son knows in his heart that Peja meant that pass for HIM.

By the way, the Kings lost the game. That bothered my son, but he talked about "the pass" all the way home.

"When I make it to the NBA, I'm going to pass the ball to kids," my son said. "And when they pass it back, I'm going to swish it, just like Peja."

Pro athletes get a bad rap and some of them deserve it. But when a star athlete makes a small gesture to brighten a young fan's day—especially when that kid is celebrating his birthday—people should know about it.

When a good guy does something great like this, it shouldn't go unnoticed.

Lessons Of Life And Love Learned Off The Court

Most kids hate homework. It's an educational fact of life. I'm sure there are a few of you parents out there with children who can't wait to get home from school, dunk a few Oreo cookies in a cold glass of milk and start on those fractions.

If you are one of those parents, I envy you.

My kids are the other kind, the kind who despise turning off their Rugrats or Sponge Bob Squarepants cartoons or putting the basketball down to start chipping away at that book report on "The Call of the Wild" that's hanging over their heads. I mean, how can someone possibly care who started the California missions and where they placed them when a *Fresh Prince of Bel Air* rerun is on, especially if it's that funny episode where Will and Carlton get caught trying to sneak out of the mansion and go to a school dance?

Me? I love homework…for the most part…at least now any way. It's a necessary part of education, as long as it's not dumped on kids by the truckload. It's not that I look forward to sitting at the kitchen table while my kids try to multiply fractions, but I do believe homework reinforces everything they're trying to learn.

Homework is good…even when it doesn't come from school.

All three of my boys are attending the winter basketball camp at Elk Grove High School. Varsity coach Dan Goldman, his assistants and players run the program. My oldest son has attended the Thundering Herd camp for years and he gets a lot out of it. I see his rebounding and shooting skills improve with each camp. Like most kids, he still needs to keep working on his defense and cut down on launching 30-foot jumpers. But what I like most about this camp is the "homework" assignment passed out on the first day.

Campers sit attentively on the hardwood floor of Elk Grove High's Bill Cartwright gym. They soak in every word, eager to absorb explanations about the intricacies of the sport. Hopefully, they'll get a lot out of learning the proper way to defend a ball handler or box out an opponent to snag a rebound. But I'm hoping it's that special "homework" assignment that the kids will appreciate and benefit from the most.

"When you go home, I want you to hug you mother, give her a kiss and tell her how much you love her," Coach Goldman told the campers. "I want you to make her cry."

The idea is to teach the boys and girls to thank their parents for forking over the money to attend camp and providing the weekly transportation to the gym to help them become better basketball players. However, it goes far beyond that. They will continue to shoot hoops during recess, many of them will make their elementary school teams, eventually some of them might make their high school basketball squads and a small portion of them will play ball in college. But the notion behind the "love assignment" is to teach the young players that what matters most in life is family. Long after the buzzer sounds and the crowd stops cheering, the Moms and Dads will be there to either congratulate or comfort, or both, both on and off the court.

My sons completed their assignments during mass at church. Of course, just like at home, I had to remind them of their unfinished work. I reminded them that Coach said he would ask the parents if their children did what they were supposed to do. You can't look a coach straight in the eye and tell a fib.

"Go over to Mom and finish the homework Coach Goldman gave you," I whispered.

One by one, they walked over to my wife, hugged her and whispered something in her ear. By the third hug, my wife's eyes turned red and her face became a little flushed.

"What did you say to her?" I asked my eight-year-old son, the final hugger of the group.

"I told her she was priceless to me," he smiled.

GRAPPLING WITH THE WRESTLING ISSUE

It is called "Smackdown!" And I hate it. It's one of those wrestling shows on television where chest pounding, beefy men whip each other around inside a ring while shocked announcers bark out phrases like: "I can't believe he's getting away with that!" or "How much of a beating must one man take before someone steps in to stop that guy's torso from being torn to shreds?"

Wrestling is not what you'd call intellectual entertainment. If you're looking for cerebral dialogue and intricate plot lines, "Smackdown!" is **not** for you. It's kind of like the Jenny Jones Show only without the insightful exploration of many of today's important issues such as sleeping with in-laws, cross-dressing and "You Made Fun of Me in High School but Look at Me Now!"

(Writer's note: That last sentence was sarcastic and not meant to be taken seriously.)

Plain and simple, "Smackdown!" is a performance, complete with rock music and flashing lights. Our three boys watched about ten minutes of it once in our house and we told them that was ten minutes too much. They whined and demanded to know why they are banned from viewing a show that many of their friends watch. Our reasoning was simple: the show—in our opinion—is stupid.

But our reason for not allowing the kids to watch some guy who calls himself "Mankind" go against some other huge guy like "Stone Cold Steve Austin" is more than just the stupidity factor. It's hyped up violence wrapped around screaming giants and scantily clad women who are surrounded by blood thirsty fans owning a collective IQ that is lower than plant life. (Then again, that's only my opinion.)

Yet, even though our kids cannot watch this show, they know all about it. They come home from school filled with glorious stories of "The Godfather" and "The Rock" leaping around the ring. There are women wearing bikinis and high heels, pulling each other's hair. Wrestlers yell at the audience and make obscene gestures. Many of their school buddies are faithful "Smackdown!" fans and fill them in on every raunchy detail.

It's not your ideal thought of family entertainment.

Coca-Cola recently body slammed the wrestling industry when the wealthy corporation said it would no longer advertise with the World Wrestling Federation's (WWF) "Smackdown!" show. A Coke executive said the show was going too far. Too much sexuality. Too many obscene gestures. Both the Air Force and the Army also suspended advertising with the WWF. The decisions by these sponsors won't have the WWF financially pinned to the mat but other sponsors also are stepping into the ring.

However, the WWF promised to reform and that had my boys excited. They saw the headline of a newspaper article stating that wrestling officials pledged to tone down their programming.

"Dad! They promised to change! Now can we watch it?"

"Sorry, guys. No way."

I had to tell them they'd still have to keep getting their WWF education from buddies at school or in the neighborhood. We're still going to keep it out of our house. I explained that even though the WWF folks promised to lighten up a little that it does not take away from the fact that the whole thing is stupid. (Again, that's only my opinion.)

There's already enough wrestling going on in my house. I don't need to have my three boys getting inspired while watching sweaty, tattoo covered, 300-pound men pound each other. Our neighbors must already think we have a wrestling ring in our house by the way it shakes and by the sounds coming from it:

"Get off my head!"

"Then you let go of my leg!"

"That's not my leg. That's yours."

"Oh."

I have to admit, I am a reformed wrestling fan. When I was a kid, I used to watch what was called "Studio Wrestling" nearly every Saturday night…with my grandmother. Grandma used to love watching Bruno Sammartino take on Johnny "The Hurricane" Hunt while "The Batman" waited in the wings. But if Grandma were alive today, she'd be offended by the way wrestling has evolved.

Grandma wouldn't like the swearing, the obscene gestures and the sexuality. She wouldn't go for the crotch grabbing grapplers with their hands all over the implant wearing cuties parading around the ring. However, Granny would still approve of chair tossing, eye gouging and illegal double-teaming when the referee isn't looking. Those things are timeless standards.

I guess if it's a show your Grandma cannot watch…even if it's wrestling…then it's not worth watching.

A Crash Course In Sports

My wife grew up in a family of five girls. None of them were very athletic or interested in sports. For them, the word "bunt" was probably short for buntcake. "Stealing" that was encouraged and carried no serious consequences was just plain wrong. "Backfield in motion" was no doubt inappropriate…but the suggestion of it probably made them a little curious.

The five daughters watched Sunday afternoon football with their Dad but after a quarter or two they'd get bored and, one by one, leave the room. They didn't play softball or soccer growing up. Some of the sisters—my wife included—gave the swim team a shot but hung up their goggles after the water got a bit too chilly on winter mornings.

My wife tried out for cheerleading in the eighth grade but didn't make it. Getting cut from the squad while some of her friends made it was a tragically sad experience. Our family knows the saga all too well because it's a tale my wife often recounts when compelled to offer an example of "life's disappointments." The kids roll their eyes when they hear the familiar cheerleading story but they politely listen. I always try to compliment them on at least presenting the illusion that they're interested.

I may have to start offering bribes—cash prizes, vacation trips—to insure their tolerance of the "I didn't make the cheerleading team but it doesn't mean I'm a bad person or a failure" story. The older they get, the more it's going to cost me.

Anyway, the point I'm trying to make is this: my wife has never had a great interest in sports, but she's a great sport when it comes to our kids. She stands on the sidelines or sits in the bleachers and shouts words of encouragement. She slaps high fives after great athletic achievements and provides sympathetic embraces after poor performances. In fact, our extensive research shows that a Butterfinger Blizzard from Dairy Queen is the perfect answer for an absolutely lousy day on the soccer field or the basketball court. And they're good for the children too.

Despite my wife's lack of knowledge or real interest in sports, we did have a breakthrough one evening after an entire season of watching our oldest son play for the Kerr Middle School seventh grade basketball team. She went to his games and cheered her head off with the other parents before gathering up the nerve to ask our son: "So, what position do you play? Exactly what are you supposed to do?"

It took several months but we finally had a breakthrough. She was ready for a crash course in sports.

She understood the main objectives of basketball are 1) scoring more baskets than your opponent and 2) preventing your opponent from scoring. But now she was ready to reach the next level of sports enlightenment.

"I play wing or guard but sometimes I'm a forward," our seventh grader answered.

"What do wings and forwards do?"

My son's eyes lit up as he assumed the role of teacher. He launched into a long explanation of his position and the duties involved and my wife transformed into a sponge. She wanted to understand a lot more.

"What are you supposed to do when you run plays?" she asked.

The floodgates opened!

The next thing my wife knew, one of the kids pulled out a white board and a black erasable marker. Suddenly, all three of our basketball loving boys were illustrating plays and explaining the difference between power forwards and centers. They covered the board with X's, O's and squiggly lines.

The session seemed to run for an hour. The more questions my wife asked, the more excited the boys became.

"What positions do Chris Webber and Shaquille O'Neil play?"

"What's a point guard and a shooting guard?"

By the end of the session my wife had a better handle on the pick and roll. She's still struggling with the man to man defense versus the zone…but all in due time.

The whole episode of Basketball 101 was great to watch. The boys were connecting with their Mom like never before. She was there when they all learned to walk, when they all learned the alphabet, when they all trotted off to school for the first time. But THEY were there when she learned about the double pick. The fact that they were teaching HER something gave the boys a feeling of satisfaction.

Now when my wife watches our boys play basketball, she watches with more understanding. She can tell the difference between a mugging and a good steal as the result of a strong double-teaming.

But all this newfound knowledge will never replace a mother's intuition. Even after filling her brain with all this basketball knowledge, she still knows that a hug and a quarter pounder with cheese are good for what ails a hoopster who failed to perform up to his own expectations. That is a basketball-related skill that is instinctive to any mother.

BASKETBALL: NOT ALWAYS THE SPORT OF BROTHERLY LOVE

The trash talking was endless. Being at the dinner table was like sitting courtside at an NBA game (like anyone who's not Jack Nicholson can really afford to do that) and listening to opposing players try to get under each others skin. The posturing grew overbearing to the point that it was beyond amusing. That's what it's like when you have two sons who faced the possibility of opposing each other in a basketball tournament.

If you have children with even a casual interest in basketball, then you've might have heard of the "Hoop It Up" tournament. It's a three-on-three basketball competition that's held every year at local college campuses across the country. Players—of all age groups—from all over the region play against competitors from the same age groups.

My twelve-year-old son and some of his six grade classmates geared up and gathered their version of The Dream Team. And they were just too cool for words. They called themselves the "Hoopsterz". The "z" at the end was for style. They'd played in a few other tournaments and managed to not humiliate themselves or become seriously injured, so they wanted to try it again. Gotta give them credit. Lose a handful of games by huge margins and to have the courage to do it all over again, well…that's kind of foolish. But they wanted to try any way. The Hoopsterz had specific plays worked out. (Some, if executed properly, would actually lead to scores.) They had practices scheduled. (We're told the plan was to put down the Nintendo controllers and actually practice.)

My ten-and-a-half year old son was also anxious to play, but he had no team. He's the typical middle child, always competing with the big brother. The fact that he wasn't on a team was deflating his little brother ego.

"Too bad. Maybe next year," the older brother chuckled with no trace of sympathy in his voice. In fact, sympathy was the furthest thing from his mind. What was on his mind was giving younger brother a huge ration of "you know what".

However, there was a twist of fate, that my wife and I believe was an act of divine intervention designed to intensify our family dynamics. (As if we needed intensifying.) Some other sixth grade boys asked my middle son— A FIFTH GRADER—to join their team. To him this was on the level of having a high school basketball player be invited to try out for the pros, except that there weren't millions of dollars or shoe contracts involved. He jumped (no basketball pun intended) at the chance to play, especially if it meant possibly challenging big brother.

The name my younger son's team chose was "Rage." Surely a group of grade school kids called "Rage", sporting t-shirts with the sleeves cut off to accentuate their bony arms would strike fear into the hearts of opponents everywhere.

The moment the younger brother joined his team, the climate in our household got chillier. The furnace automatically clicked on every time both basketballers were in the same room. Neither ballplayer talked about their practices or their plays or their teammates for fear of divulging super-secret plays designed to demolish opponents.

ME: "How was practice son?"

OLDER SON: "Fine."

ME: "Working on some new plays?"

OLDER SON: Yeah. (Eyes shifting to middle son) Sure.

ME: (Speaking to the middle son) How'd your practice go?

MIDDLE SON: Good. (Eyes shifting to older brother) No, great! That's what I meant…GREAT!

At first, the trash talking was subtle, with little jabs at each other's team-mates and their alleged weaknesses. Then it got ugly in a comical kind of way.

"Don't bother showing up if we're on your schedule! We'll kill you guys!"

"Yeah. I heard they're starting your team in the LOSER'S bracket to save time!"

The kid from "Rage" and the one from the "Hoopsterz" went verbally one-on-one for weeks. "Friendly games" of hoops outside usually ended in shouting matches with one of them being "lucky" while the other was the "sore loser."

When the big tournament finally came, my wife and I were more anxious than the boys. We wanted the head-to-head competition more than they did. We wanted to see how both of them could stand up to it all.

Unfortunately, their teams were in different divisions. They ended up battling other kids instead of beating up on each other like we had hoped. There's nothing like a friendly brotherly bloodletting to make life interesting. They were disappointed, but my wife and I were even more so. We wanted to see the younger brother handle the pressure of facing the big brother that he looks up to. We also wanted to see the older son react to possibly losing to the kid brother that he somewhat admires, but won't admit.

The rumble on the court will have to wait for another day. Until then, we will just have to settle for listening to the trash talk about what might have been.

I Don't Want To Play

It's going to be a very different kind of spring and summer. I'm going to miss the smell of the freshly trimmed grass and the clank of the aluminum bat and the hard slide into second base. I'm going to miss sitting in the dugout with the hot, afternoon sun baking the back of my neck. I'm going to miss spitting sunflower seeds from the top of the grandstands and hoping that they fall onto the fresh dirt below, and not on someone's nachos.

Those are the little things about youth league baseball that I'll miss the most this year.

My boys have decided to take a baseball sabbatical. They won't be competing in the Cal Ripken League this season. We're putting the gloves and the spikes on the shelf for a while. As a family, we've come close to our breaking point. We've hit the wall, so to speak. My wife and I are dealing with our own jobs along with the insanity of trying to shuttle our four kids to all of their activities: flag football and karate lessons and basketball camp and soccer. And let's not forget all the schoolwork that was getting pushed to the back burner! That's just not acceptable.

We reached our burnout point. The kids did, too. We faced the truth…you just can't do everything.

The average day has a limited number of hours. Having a laundry list of extra activities left the kids with less and less time to just be kids. Some things had to give. We gave them options. What they could continue and what they could cancel. Not playing baseball was their decision to make.

And it was a tough one for me to take.

I grew up with baseball and baseball helped me grow up. I played the game until my twenties and it was always a big part of my life. It's kind of hard for me to accept the fact that it won't be such a big part of their lives. We all need to adjust. Especially me.

However, the calendar magnetically clinging to the refrigerator never seems to have any empty days on it. Almost every day it's blocked out, almost to the minute. We're all about a half-inch away from going over the deep end trying to keep up this frantic pace. Dinner comes later and later. We're eating too much fast food. Homework that they just don't have time to complete *before* their activities gets their attention *after*, but it only makes the days seem longer and it compounds the stress. We're not reading enough bedtime stories.

We've been running into too many situations where there's too much to do and not enough time to do it. The kids have increasingly less time to just have fun doing nothing.

We've always believed in keeping kids busy, but we have reached that "too busy" point, that critical mass. After a full day of school, the kids are still running in fifth gear, sometimes until 8:00pm, several nights a week. We needed to call a time out.

There's a lot of value in unstructured time and the kids have very little of it.

So, baseball is out. At least for a while. Maybe even for good and that makes me feel bad. I'm going to miss hopping up and down inside the third base coach's box and frantically waving my arm in windmill fashion, as if acting like a maniac could actually get a kid safely home. And then there's the cool, Delta breeze skimming along the treetops in the evening as the opposing players high five each other at the end of each game. I'm also actually going to miss the grossed out feeling I get that comes from finding catcher's cups in interesting and inappropriate places in the house.

I love baseball, but my kids shouldn't play the sport just because they think I want them to play. Don't play for me, I tell them. Play for yourselves. Find the things you really want to dedicate time to and do it. Just don't overdo it.

If you try packing too much into life you might miss too many things along the way.

ECONOMICS

"A man can't get rich if he takes proper care of his family."

Navaho saying

"Blessed are the young for they shall inherit the national debt."

Herbert Hoover

If The Shoe Fits It Must Have Cost You A Fortune

There are few simple choices any more. If you order a burger, you must decide between the single, the double, the one with special sauce, or go with onion rings and bacon. Then, what about supersizing?

At coffee bars you have to strain your eyes at the menu to find a plain cup of java. You can get mocha, or a mochachino, or a latte. Then that leads to the frustrating question: single shot or double shot of espresso?

Too many choices…which naturally leads me to the subject of basketball shoes.

When I was a kid, we had only a few choices. We had the Chuck Taylor Converse All-Star in black, or white, high top or low top. If your parents didn't want to spend the money (around twenty bucks back then) you settled for P.F. Flyers which was like wearing the scarlet letter. Converse were for cool kids. P.F. Flyers were for goobers.

The Flyers commercials always featured some kid lacing up the sneakers, then racing and leaping over the camera with promises that you would "run faster and jump higher." This statement was made long before anyone cared about truth in advertising. The geeks who relied on the Flyers for help were usually disappointed to learn the not-so-miraculous shoes were nothing but canvas and rubber. The magic must have been sold separately.

When I made the eighth grade basketball team at St. Joseph's, my parents sprang for the black, high-top, All-Stars. There were two reasons for the purchase: I begged, and also a previous P.F. experiment failed miserably. When I made the junior varsity team my sophomore year, my parents sprang for a pair of red Pumas. They had even less of an impact on my

79

athletic performance as the P.F. Flyers, but the Puma people never made promises.

Now, I have three boys who are crazy about basketball. My oldest made the seventh grade team at his middle school. My middle son made the grade school team at his elementary school. My youngest son isn't old enough to compete on the school team. He plays in a recreational league. And I have found that as crazy as they are about basketball, they are even crazier about basketball shoes.

At games, they watch the players rebound and shoot, and they scout out the player's feet.

"Look, that one has the new Jordans!"

"Oh yeah, and check out the Iversons on that one! Those are tight!"

(Translation: when a kid says "tight" that means, "cool", not "too small.")

Anyway, my middle son wanted a certain type of shoe for Christmas. It was all he asked for this year.

"I want the Nike Air Force Authority shoes in red," he pleaded. He did his research and knew this was the shoe to end all shoes.

So, my wife and I went on a quest for this special shoe, which made no special promises. The problem was that we couldn't find a nearby store that carried them. Stores had the Nike Boys Jordan Retro XI or the Nike Kids Air Electrifying Max. If he didn't want those, he could pick the Adidas Superstar Metal Chaos or the And 1 Postgametochillin model. But NO…it had to be the Air Force Authority.

It seems only one retailer chain carries this model. The closest store with that extraordinary model was in a city about a thirty-minute drive from our home. We made the trek there, but they didn't have THE shoe.

We went online to order from the company…but they were out of stock.

We searched. We made calls. We did everything but send out a search party. Finally, we found another store that had these stupid shoes. This store was in another city, a forty-five minute drive in the other direction.

We piled into the minivan and blasted off on our mission like a space shuttle crew jetting off on an important expedition. We made it to the mall in record time, although no speed limit laws were broken. I swear. We found the blasted shoes and pounced on them like a scrappy guard diving for a loose ball.

Now, my son is happy. He loves his shoes and is grateful for the gift. We logged a lot of miles and used about two tanks of gas finding the sneakers. They weren't outrageously expensive, so we can justify the cost.

But it made me wonder, if the same player tried both, let's say, the Adidas Superstar Nebulas and the white Chuck Taylor Converse All-Stars would there be much of a difference in his performance? Maybe not, but it could effect his attitude. And I guess, on the court, attitude is everything.

THE COSTLY COST OF LIVING WITH CHILDREN

They surround you. They stalk you like a lion lurking in the high brush, poised to pounce. They look for the weak moments, those moments when they sense that your guard is down. It is the smell of blood…the smell of fear that draws them closer. And then…they strike.

"Dad, I need twenty dollars for a school field trip!"

"Dad, basketball sign-ups are gonna run around sixty-five bucks and I need some new shorts too!"

"Dad, the new Michael Jordans are out. What's the limit on the charge card these days?"

"Daddy, I know I just got these new jeans but those jeans at Mervyns are really cute and…."

And when they leave, I am left sitting on the couch with my wallet open, empty and smoldering. I am dazed and wondering what just hit me. Just like all those people who live in the Midwest describe a tornado—"It sounded like a freight train coming"—my four children pick my pockets with about as much poise as some type of natural disaster.

In case you haven't noticed, kids are expensive creatures to have around the house. They keep requiring larger quantities of food. Their clothing—at least the garments that don't get torn to shreds from normal daily wear—never fits two months after the purchase. The costs of their activities add up. They don't eat Happy Meals any more. Only the super-sized value meals will do, and maybe more than one will be necessary to fill them up. Throw in the need for an occasional doctor's visit and prescription and the adding machine keeps clicking away.

A friend recently sent us an e-mail that quoted some government study stating that raising a child from birth to age 18 costs roughly $160,140 for the average middle income family. That just didn't sound right. It seemed like a little on the high side to me! I know kids are high-priced. I know that based on personal experiences…and the aforementioned smoldering wallet, for instance. But to think that raising a child all those years would cost THAT much left me doubtfully curious.

So I decided to do some calculating of my own. I searched the Internet and came across one of those "cost of living" calculators from an investment company website. It gave cost estimates for everything from groceries to children's activities to the ever popular "miscellaneous." I filled in all the blanks, deleted the spots that didn't apply—like day care and babysitting since my wife's work schedule helps us avoid those costs—and then clicked the "total" button.

Turns out that I was right. The trusty *"here's how much your kids are costing you"* calculator told me that raising one of my children would NOT cost a staggering $160,140. According to the number crunching, raising a Herrera kid will cost us a measly $157,900! What a bargain! That's less than the government's guess, but we get to increase the agony a little in our house. If you are like us, multiply that figure times the number of children you have. In our case, multiply the estimate by four and you come up with a grand total for us of $631,600.

Ouch!

Do the math! I just did it and hurt myself.

That's a lot of money for food, clothing, braces, baseball gloves, hair gel, ponytail holders, books, occasional movie tickets, and art supplies. But on the flip side, it's a bargain when you consider the deal also includes tucking them in at night, watching them perform in the school play, treating skinned knees, explaining why some kids get invited to birthday parties when others don't, and hopefully dancing at their wedding while wiping the tears from your eyes.

Even though it's all pretty pricey, it's all worth the price. Now, they will still sense when you are at your weakest of moments, slyly stalk you and pounce. Only from now on, you have to put up a better fight hanging onto that wallet since you've done the math and know what kind of financial damage the kids can do.

Back To School, Break The Bank

It's Back-To-School season. Do you want to know how I can tell? It's not because of all the sales or the steady motorcade of bright yellow buses rolling through Elk Grove or from my instinctive impulsive desire to shove all of the children out of the house by 7:45 a.m. every Monday through Friday. I can tell it is Back-To-School season based on the huge dent in the family checking account. The dent is so large it leaves a bruise.

It's a seasonal thing. Come late August or early September, massive amounts of hard-earned money disappear from the minimal amount we manage to squirrel away. The cash vanishes in chunks. It's more expensive than Christmas, but not as costly as if you forgot your wedding anniversary.

We have four kids. Two of them attend an elementary school where they are required to wear uniforms. Our two older children attend a middle school where they are required to wear clothing that cost infinitely more than a few sets of navy blue shorts and white pullover golf shirts. Well, they are not "required" to wear such clothing. It just turns out that the clothing they want just happens to be more expensive than uniforms.

My wife reluctantly took our older boys on a shopping spree that included Old Navy and the brand name shops that make up the Folsom outlet stores. An outlet center is a place where name brand stores get together in one location, charge a few cents less for their products knowing that you are now spending twice as much money on gasoline to save a nickel on a pair of shoes. The boys came back home with large shopping bags and huge smiles on their faces. My wife returned home tired, broke and dejected knowing that the Back-To-School spending splurge was far from over while the checkbook was telling her it was time to cease and desist!

We still had to procure a ton of school necessities and that somehow landed us at Wal-Mart. And the folks there are smart. They have provided dazed parents with a pre-made shopping list of items that 7th and 8th graders need to start the school year. The Wal-Mart list includes the following necessities: back pack, three-ring binder, rulers, scissors, erasers, paper clips, paper punch, hi-lighters, tablets and tote bags.

Good thinking Wal-Mart! But if you truly want to help the parents of middle schoolers and high school students there are a few other items that we need to tack onto the list. How about ridiculously expensive t-shirts that are made out of the same material as your general underwear, but cost much, much more because of the brand name emblazoned across the front?

The Back-To-School shopping list should also include high-priced sneakers that cost the same as a car payment. Not only do these shoes have to be pricey; they either have to be a Nike product or a brand endorsed by a professional athlete with either a criminal record, or a body covered with tattoos.

Also, anything bearing the name "Abercrombie & Fitch" is also acceptable. Anything. Absolutely anything.

Then you have to consider pants. The pants must be slightly oversized and have ten million pockets, perfect for misplacing lunch money, neatly folded up homework assignments or ballpoint pens that eventually show up in the laundry.

My wife and I are grateful that school starts but once a year, because the kids keep growing, styles and fashions keep changing and prices keep rising. If we start saving money now, we might have enough cash packed away in time for the kids to say, "Oh, please! Abercrombie & Fitch is so twenty-minutes ago!"

THE SEARCH FOR THE ELUSIVE SILVER EGG

"I got it! Now all of you must bow down to me," my oldest son, a seventh grader said as his younger siblings looked on with envy.

It was Easter and he held the elusive silver egg over his head like an Olympian coveting a glorious gold medal. Indiana Jones had just reached the Temple of Doom and left his treasure hungry competitors in the dust.

This time, the prized possession was not equal to the Dead Sea Scrolls or some kind of moss covered vase. It was only a silver plastic egg containing a five-dollar bill, but in our house it's a great annual prize that is to be coveted.

We have an Easter tradition. And although we are fairly religious people, and attend mass every Sunday and on our church's special days, this certain tradition is not of an enormously religious nature and probably not greatly promoted by the Vatican. We take plastic eggs, stuff money inside them, and hide the riches throughout the house for our kids to find. We use money because chocolate eggs can melt and wreck the rug. And the dog can sniff out the candy and also—within time—wreck the rug. Real eggs get stinky if undetected for too long and, of course; there is the dog and her rug wrecking ability to consider again.

The night before Easter, my wife and I cram coins, and a few dollar bills, inside a pile of plastic eggs. While the kids sleep, we hide the tiny plastic treasure chests throughout our home. Some eggs contain a few nickels; some contain up to a dollar. However, the Holy Grail of plastic eggs is silver and contains the grandest of grand prizes…a five-dollar bill. The silver egg finder is the supreme winner of the quest.

The money hunt in our Elk Grove, California home is a carryover from my wife's childhood in Pittsburgh, Pennsylvania. She was one of five girls and every Easter—along with a basket of candy—her parents hid money-filled plastic eggs throughout their house. On Easter mornings, the daughters stampeded through the house, trampling furniture and siblings in an effort to bag the most cash.

"By the time we were in college, we needed the spending money," my wife says, retelling our children every year.

This year, our children were looking forward to the annual challenge of capturing the coveted silver egg. We pumped them up for several days, like enthusiastic college coaches getting players ready for that big bowl game.

You gotta want the egg. You gotta see the egg. You gotta be the egg.

Personally, I hoped it would go undetected, in case I needed lunch money some day.

We told the kids that they couldn't get out bed before 7:30 on Easter morning. Of course, the egg free-for-all was in full swing by 6:58 a.m. By around 7:30, the kids had collected every egg…except the most desired one.

It wasn't long before three of our four young hunters had enough. The rush for cash took a lot out of them, but our oldest—a penny conscious penny pincher—refused to quit. The challenge of the hunt—not to mention the dough—inspired him to press on.

He asked for hints. Was he hot or cold? Was he close? Is the egg in the downstairs closet, in his underwear drawer or on the roof? We weren't going to make the pursuit that easy for him.

We told him to think like Steve Foster, that crazy Australian Crocodile Hunter from Animal Planet who will pick up venomous creatures and say things like, "Isn't she a beauty?" We told our son that animal lover Steve would find our hiding place to be "a beauty!"

That was his hint.

Our son started thinking "animal". He searched the dog's bed. No egg.

The pet rat cage! Wait a minute. No. We wouldn't put a prized egg in a cage with a rodent and his steady supply of droppings.

Continuing with the animal clue, he searched the 100-pound sack of dog food without success. While the other kids sat watching cartoons, satisfied with their measly loose change, the relentless Egg Hunter continued hunting for hours. He was not about to quit until he had bagged his prize.

Inside our garage is one of the ugliest pieces of "artwork" that you'll ever find. It is a macramé owl that somehow we inherited from a friend who must have felt that it wasn't quite right for their home. (What is *that* supposed to tell you?) It hangs in our garage above the garbage can, perhaps to scare away the flies. Inside the beak of the macramé owl was lodged the very shiny silver egg and its very green five-dollar yolk.

Our son grabbed the prize and claimed victory. He strutted into the family room with his head—and the egg—held high. I tried feeling happy for him, but I could not because I had lost my emergency lunch money to the triumphant Egg Hunter.

GROWING OLDER

"It's not what you do for your children, but what you have taught them to do for themselves that will make them successful human beings."

Ann Landers

"The old believe everything, the middle-aged suspect everything, the young know everything."

Oscar Wilde

Putting Perspective On Middle-Age Life

I sat in my car at the red light, studying the man in the car next to me, wondering which one of us had the true perspective on life. That is, if there is such a thing. I didn't know the guy, had no idea how he reached this point in his life, so it seemed unfair to make judgments, but I did so anyway.

The contrast I was making in my mind lasted only a few seconds at an intersection in Elk Grove on a blistering summer day. And it made me realize that the question: "Where am I?" doesn't always deal with geography.

This guy and I appeared to be the same age, but I was trying to figure out which one of us was actually older…if you know what I mean?

My trusty green 1994 Saturn, with a hearty layer of dust, faced the same direction as his silver, right out of the showroom, convertible. My air conditioner shot cool air as the radio played rock tunes from a station that makes my kids groan. (Today's kids don't appreciate high-pitched guitar licks or drum solos that last longer than a drive to the mall.) The guy next to me had the top down; the intense sunlight was baking his skin. My music competed with the hip, alternative rock that flowed from what was probably a multiple CD changer pumping sound through six state-of-the-art speakers.

My sensible golf shirt—that either came from Mervyn's or Costco—matched my shorts. I know this because my wife bought the pair together. He wore his sleeveless t-shirt at the appropriate angle as to leave his tattoo visible to the public. It was either a picture of a fire breathing dragon or Bob Marley. I couldn't tell. The man's baseball cap—worn backwards—kept the wind from mussing his collar length hair.

The only thing we appeared to have in common was that we both were wearing our seatbelts.

I wondered about this guy my age. Did *his* knees creak when he stands up? Were his sunglasses prescription and, if so, were they bifocals? If he ate Mexican food too late in the evening, did it keep *him* up at night?

I wondered all of these things because I have a birthday approaching. When you are middle-aged and you have a birthday approaching you are supposed to look at life introspectively. At least, that's what they do on sit-coms and in movies.

You may be wondering how I'm starting to realize I'm getting older:

- When people call after 10:00pm, they ask: "Did I wake you?"
- When we have parties at our house the neighbors don't notice.
- The instrumental music playing in elevators is not only familiar to me; I know the songs by name.
- I get into lengthy discussions about health insurance, 401Ks and utility bills.
- Nice looking clothes are important to me, but comfortably fitting clothes are more important.

Again, without trying to be judgmental (although I am failing here), I imagined what the motorist beside me didn't have; a wife like mine, beautiful, loving and amazingly tolerant.

Maybe his kids didn't bring home great grades and didn't allow hugs in public. Maybe he didn't have a job where he talks with interesting people every day.

Back at the intersection, the light turned green, and I drove straight ahead. My new friend punched the accelerator and turned right. I doubt that he gave the green Saturn and the guy inside a second thought and I should regard the fellow in the convertible the same way.

When I was younger there was this TV program called "Then Came Bronson." It was about a motorcycle-riding drifter. In the open of the show, Bronson sat at a red light revving his customized Harley-Davidson Sportster motorcycle. Next to him was a guy driving a beat-up station wagon. The two exchanged looks and the station wagon guy nodded his head, in a manner that suggested that he admired and wanted to emulate Bronson's carefree lifestyle.

What a bunch of baloney!

The non-geographical question, "Where am I?" can have whatever answer you give it. As my birthday approaches, the best answer to that question is "Where I am supposed to be!"

Finding The Right Father's Day Gift From The Heart

You're probably thinking about neckties right about now. If you're not, you should be. Father's Day is just around the corner. I always say that because it always is around the corner at some point during the year. If you are thinking about ties, go for something bright and bold. Sears most likely has a sale on underwear, t-shirts and socks. Words to the wise…think durability when it comes to undergarments. Men like underwear with endurance. Consider searching through Target's sporting goods section, or maybe you can pick some CDs that *you* really want, but can pass along as presents.

Whatever you choose, please remember to choose wisely as Father's Day approaches because it is rapidly approaching…sooner or later.

Personally, I love receiving shirts and ties. My closet is proof that I am a Dad with four giving children and one loving and generous wife. My desk is decorated with picture frames and mouse pads celebrating past Father's Days. You should see the coffee mugs. My collection would make Ward Cleaver envious.

I wish I could give my Dad a Father's Day gift, but I haven't been able to for several years. Dad died eight years ago, the victim of health problems and hard work. And even though toward the end, shopping for something he didn't have became an escalating challenge, I miss not being able to find him a present, any present, and send it to him with a card.

So, this coming year, I'm giving him the words on these pages that he'll probably read after showing off the book cover to my Uncle Joe and Saint Peter. (I'm hoping that that Saint Peter doesn't mind that he has to wait his turn after my uncle.)

- Being a father is sometimes a thankless position in the family and if I never thanked you for having that post and all the headaches that go with it, I'd like to thank you now. I don't know how you retained even a shred of sanity knowing what my sister and I put you through.

- I never could get the curveball to stop hanging over the middle of the plate. I could never throw that pitch well enough to get past small college baseball. But it wasn't because you did a lousy job teaching. As Dirty Harry once said: "A man's got to know his limitations."

- On my 21st birthday, I should have taken you out for a beer and invited along Uncle Tony and Uncle Joe. It would have been a good time to share some stories. The Spotlight Lounge was only a few blocks from the house. We could have walked.

- I should have mowed the lawn more often. And trimmed the hedges. And pruned the trees. And shoveled the sidewalk during those frigid Western Pennsylvania winters. You just always did those unwelcome jobs yourself without asking. Sorry for not volunteering.

- That scratch in your new Ford Grand Torino…well…I did that. A renegade shopping cart roaring around the Super Dollar parking lot was not to blame.

- That time you cried when you and Mom dropped me off at college for the first time, I should have hugged you "goodbye" longer. It really didn't hit me until after you drove off what that moment must have meant to you. As my kids get older, I'm learning the value of those moments.

- Whether you realized it or not, I did appreciate your stories about laboring in the steel mills and I did get something out of them. Hearing how back breakingly hard it was being a bricklayer helped convince me that pursuing college was the best path for me. It paid off.

• And thanks for sticking around long enough for me to say goodbye to you one last time. That's probably the moment that I both
greatly cherish and intensely dislike at the same time.

These are just all little tidbits gathered along the way that helped shape
me, good bad or indifferent. And I think that while you are all roaming
the aisles of the nearest bookstore or bargain center for that perfect gift,
pick up some nice things that Dad will like. But remember that saying
thanks to your father for what seem like insignificant moments right now
can also make great gifts.

MOM'S KEYS

There's a key on my key ring that can't open anything within thousands of miles of my California home. It won't unlock my desk, or my locker or my garage. It doesn't fit any doorknob around here. The key is to my mother's home in Pennsylvania. Although, I haven't lived in that house for twenty-two years, I've always kept the key.

How could I ever get rid of it?

Pretty soon, the key won't do me any good. My mother is selling the only home she's known for the past 45 years, the house where I grew up, the house where she raised our family.

It's going to be tough…on Mom and on me.

She'll be 78 soon and she's lived by herself since my father died. Travelling alone to visit us at our house in Elk Grove and to see my sister in Phoenix is rough for her. Living alone is worse. Living alone isn't a good thing for anyone, especially your mother.

My sister's children are in college, so living with her will be easier for Mom. Our house—with four kids, two working parents, and a frenetic schedule—is "a little loud" as Mom politely puts it.

And it won't quiet down here in Elk Grove for a while.

Right now there's a real estate sign in the front yard, where I used to glide down on my sled in the dead of winter, go flying over a three foot high stone wall my father built, only to eventually bang into Mr. Herman's car, or his hedges if I was lucky. However, he was always a very understanding neighbor. He knew he could snag peaches from our tree whenever he wanted. I think I always got the better end of the deal.

My cousin the realtor is handling the sale. She posted Mom's house—my house—on the Internet and the place looks so lonely in the digital photograph posted in cyberspace. The house looks familiar, but doesn't look like it's mine any more.

Last week, two couples walked through my old house. They measured the rooms. They checked out the finished basement. They had to be impressed with the size of the lot. It's huge, big enough for a dozen kids to play tackle football and not bang into anything except the tiny vegetable garden just to the left of the garage.

No one's made an offer on the house yet. It's only a matter of time. It's a great little red brick place. A covered porch takes up the whole side of the house. On rainy spring evenings we'd sit there and talk with neighbors and watch car after car roll through the stop sign at the corner.

"Somebody's going to get killed one of these days," someone would always snarl.

However, I can safely say there has not been one traffic fatality at the corner of Woodland and Belaire in forty-five years…but we'd still appreciate it if drivers would slow down a little.

Although she's ready to move and be around family again, it's going to be tough for my Mom to leave. She raised my sister and me there in that tiny, three-bedroom, one bath place. She welcomed my Grandmother there for long visits when my Grandfather was "having one of his moods." I took Mom back to the house just a few hours after my father died. Maybe that's when it started to feel different to her there.

The toughest part for me to accept is the fact that after Mom moves I won't have a reason to go back to my hometown again. With my mother moving, the connection won't be there any more. It feels strange knowing that I might never see that place again.

The new owners, whoever they may be, should know that deer like to sneak into the yard and nibble at the garden. Birds will come looking for food in the winter because Mom's bird feeder is always open to visitors. The wild blackberry bushes over the hill, by the side yard, are always generous.

The prospective owners should also know that, although I never intend to use the key, that I am going to keep it tightly clasped to my chain. How could I ever get rid of it?

Here's To A Healthier And Happier Father's Day

Come Sunday morning, many of you Dads will be unwrapping that Popeil Pocket Fisherman—the one your kids picked out for you at the local K-Mart for 6.99 plus tax—and you'll say "I don't fish but how did you know I've had my eye on this baby?"

Or you'll walk into your closet and find that someone has already installed the "Automatic Tie Rack" by Sharper Image. For only $39.95—plus tax—with the press of a button, your neckties parade past you while hanging from a small conveyer belt, speeding up the clothing selection process in the morning.

Or while you sit in the backyard with your feet propped up, sipping a potentially lethally strong cup of coffee one of the kids brewed for you, while another offspring zigzags across the lawn behind the mower...you'll reflect on all that's good. And you should.

When Father's Day comes, all of us Dads need to work on erasing all the things we're doing wrong with our kids and concentrate on the things that we are doing right with them. We need to keep doing those "right things" to build better relationships with them. At the same time, we need to reflect on our past and present relationships with our own fathers. It turns out that it's all good for our health and could eventually impact the health of our children.

The Journal of the American Medical Association recently completed a study about past childhoods. The study found that those who had adverse childhood and adolescent experiences and have not made peace with those events suffer from a high risk factor of heart disease, cancer and other life threatening illnesses. The study also said that people who had traumatic childhoods—especially at the hands of their fathers—survive six to seven years less than the average person does.

There's a psychologist named Harold Bloomfield who has written a bunch of books and articles on family relationships. In an online chat session with WebMD, Dr. Bloomfield said, "The root cause of human suffering is the accumulation of unprocessed experiences from the past." What Bloomfield is saying is that dealing with past problems is better than forgetting about them. He's written a book titled *Making Peace with Your Past* in which he details advice on how adults can re-examine their relationships with their parents by confronting problems, rather than burying them.

"Making peace with your father, making peace with your past is a powerful catalyst for conscious evolution," Bloomfield said.

Although I am whittling this down to an over-simplification, Bloomfield's Father's Day suggestion is this: if you are visiting your Dad and feel the need to talk about past transgressions, pick the right time and then talk about it. If your father has passed away, Dr. Bloomfield suggests that you start by writing your feelings in a letter to your father that will never be mailed. The idea is to get your feelings out so that you can quit harboring any resentments or regrets. Bloomfield insists it'll help you lead a healthier life.

My father died a little more than eight years ago. His death left behind a lot of unfinished business between us. I know I shouldn't but I consider most of it my fault for not bringing things up at the right times. I should have told him when he said things that hurt my feelings, instead of barricading myself in my room. I should have said something when he could have been nicer to my mother, rather than keeping quiet. I also should have told him what I admired about him the most, about what made me proud to be his son. There was a ton of that mixed together over the years. They were all missed opportunities, but it is not too late to talk about these things or work on fixing them.

For many of us, it isn't or wasn't easy to talk with our fathers. The job ahead it to make it is easier for our own children.

Aches And Pains

I've lost a step. Actually, make that several steps. It isn't fair to say that age is creeping up on me. Let's be honest. Age is walking alongside me, with its boney-fingered hand patting me on the shoulder, urging me to try anyway. What the heck! Go ahead! Try and do what you used to do. Age says, if you need me I'll be waiting for you in the emergency room, clutching your health insurance card, ready to check you in and get you all settled.

"Dad! We need another guy for two on two. Wanna play some hoops?"

"Sure!"

I play. I hurt.

"Dad! How many chin-ups can you do?"

"I don't know. Let's see."

They rip off a dozen. I tremble through two. They go outside and play. I stay inside and rub my sore arms.

"Ouch!" and "Ooof!" are common words in my vocabulary.

Getting older is painful. Getting to the point where you realize that you can't keep up with your sons is excruciatingly painful.

Two of my boys are in junior high. The third one is not too far behind. They are all growing in size and strength. I am growing in girth and waist.

When they were tiny, we'd play football in the front yard. I'd run in slow motion to give them enough time to catch me and wrestle me to the ground. They'd fall on me and we'd all laugh. Now when we play football, I still run in slow motion because it is the only speed I have. They wrestle me to the ground. They fall on me and laugh. I groan.

"Ooof!"

To quote Dr. Zachary Smith—the whiny, bumbling stow-away from the old television series *Lost in Space*…"Oh, the pain! The pain!"

The boys know that they are finally passing me by. They are reveling in it. It all started with a quick drive to the basket and an uncontested lay-up. Another followed that drive…then another. Now it's easy to run circles around Old Dad.

Old Dad.

This past summer, I took the kids swimming at a local public pool. We were splashing around in the five-foot zone when my oldest experienced a personal epiphany. The boy is nearly as tall as I am and he reminds me of that daily. He is solid and quick and everything I wished I were when I was thirteen. I was standing in the pool, minding my own business, sucking in my own gut, when he sneaked up from behind, wrapped me in a hearty bear hug, hoisted me up in the air and body slammed me into the water.

Old Dad. Under five feet of water. Never knew what hit him. Man, that was fun Dad. Let's do it again, he says. Let's not! I gasp. If Dad dies then he can't drive home.

The older boys are at the age now where they like to physically challenge me. It's not as if they come after me with a hatchet or a barstool—I'm told that comes much later in life—like when you take away the car keys. But they like to bump and nudge me out of the way to show me that they are gaining might, and that some day my only physical defense of sitting on them will not be enough to save my out-of-shape self from humiliation at the hands of some young bucks.

This change in life has forced me to find other ways to assert myself, to let them know that I AM THE MAN…at least for a while. I have introduced a phrase that I blurt out each and every time one of the budding young studs starts positioning himself to do some bodily harm upon me. They come at me, hands moving, making noises like Jackie Chan or they're ready to pounce on me like a NFL linebacker and all I have to shout is "ECONOMIC SANCTIONS!"

It stops them dead in their tracks.

I have explained to them that while they are now faster and quicker than I am and will no doubt be stronger than me sometime within the next twenty minutes that I am in total control because the person who controls the money controls everything.

"ECONOMIC SANCTIONS! You want those new Nike Jordans? Better chill out!"

They cut their challenge short.

"You guys want me to take you to McDonald's after basketball? You'd best walk away!"

They lower their heads, turn and slink away.

As long as I control the money in this house, I can control my level of aches and pains. It won't last forever, but by the time they are at the point where my "economic sanctions" defense becomes ineffective, they should have their own children tackling them, wrestling them to the ground and laughing.

Hopefully by then I'll be able to slip the grandkids enough money that my kids will have to come up with their own form of self-defense.

SOCIETY

"Society is like the air, necessary to breathe but insufficient to live on."

George Santayana 1863-1952) Poet

"Good humor is one of the best articles of dress one can wear in society."

William Makepeace Thackeray (1811-1863) English novelist and humorist

DAWGS, PEEPS AND DADS

My life needs subtitles to help me understand it better because on any given day I feel like a tourist walking off the bus with my camera strapped around my neck while I try making sense of my surroundings.

It's in my own home where I'm having most of my trouble. The language I'm hearing sounds strangely familiar but it also seems awfully foreign at the same time. It's the way the common words are used in combination with unintelligible blurbs that confuses me.

"Ay yo Dad! Check it out! That new game we got is da bomb!" one of my sons will say.

I pause before answering, allowing the words to sink in. Then I flip through my mental "kids slang dictionary" and start translating. The process always takes longer than I would like. The wheels start spinning. My brain starts chugging like an antique rail car pulling onto rusty tracks. After a brief eternity, my mind finishes shuffling a thick stack of slang flash cards and the interpretation is complete. What my son was actually saying was: "Hey Dad, take a look at this video game we just rented from Blockbuster. It's really great!"

"I'm glad you're enjoying it, pal." I'm uncomfortable as I answer because I am not 100-percent certain that I've properly understood his remark. I've taken so long to respond that my son probably thinks there's something wrong with me. My "uncool" rating goes up a few notches.

This happens to me several times a day and the constant translating is wearing me down. Chances are that if you have children it's also happening to you. Maybe your life could use some subtitles too.

This language barrier goes beyond the stucco-covered walls of my home. I can't go anywhere without feeling like a stranger visiting a strange land. Kids cleaning up the deli at Safeway are talking about their "peeps" and "snaps" and "rides." Teens walking out of the Mega Multiplex Monster Theater talk about what's "tight" and who is "all that." It doesn't make them bad kids. It just makes them kids that I'm agonizing to understand.

The modern day English language is evolving and I am still in the Jurassic period working with stone knives and bear skins. I am forcing myself to learn this new language in order to survive. By the way, "peeps" means "friends." "Snaps" stands for "money." "Rides" refer to "cars." Something that is "tight" is "very good" and someone who is "all that" is usually someone who is in possession of good qualities.

It's tough keeping up with this developing jargon, but I've found a way to cut down on some of its usage…at least in the house. My wife and I have found that the best way to get the kids to stop using street slang is to speak to them in their own tongue. Believe me, it is a very effective way of getting them to stop.

Here's an example (with translation provided in parentheses):

ME: "What up dawgs? How y'all livin'?" (Hi guys. How are you all doing?)

SON: "Dad, stop talking like that! (Dad, stop talking like that!)

ME: "Yo, G. Don't be getting' all up in my grill!" (Come on, buddy. Please don't get angry about it.)

SON: "Dad, I'm begging you to stop!" (Seriously, you sound really stupid Dad. Quit embarrassing yourself!)

ME: "Aw-ight. We don't need no drama. Put on your kicks and go do some hoops." (Okay. We don't need to have a very serious problem here. Why don't you put on those obscenely expensive shoes we bought for you and go outside and play some basketball?)

SON: "Aaaaaaaaaaah! (Aaaaaaaaaaah!—son screams and runs out of the room.)

ME: "Peace out." (Bye.)

It is very effective. There are few things worse than a parent, especially a middle aged bald guy, talking to teens in their own words. It really does help in getting them to speak English again…at least for a short while…and at least they become reluctant to sling slang words around in your presence.

Give it a try. I gotcha back. (I'm behind you 100-percent.)

Peace out.

GIVING IN, GETTING CONNECTED, GETTING EVEN

It may have been the immortal Darth Vadar who once said; "Resistance is futile!" And I'm sure that when the evil cloaked one was zeroing in on Luke Skywalker, that while he was talking about the dark side that he was subliminally referring to cable television.

Or maybe it was The Borg from Star Trek that made that famous declaration, when it came to being sucked in by the lure of around the clock, meaningless programming. Either way, it is safe to say that we have been assimilated.

My wife and I held out against getting cable TV for years and years and years.

"Mom! Dad! How come we don't have cable? The kids down the street have cable and they're able to watch 700 channels. Well, not at the same time, but they've got all the HBOs, ESPNs and music video channels out there!"

Our kids were seriously deprived. As if cable television was as essential as air and water. As if without cable they would not be able to communicate with other kids during lunchtime. Everyone knows that the kids who can converse about "CATDOG", or the SCI-FI Channel or ESPN highlights are cool.

Not having cable made our children feel like they were outcasts. They were misfits. They were lepers. It was obvious that my wife and I were socially stifling our children.

We've always felt that it's a lot of money for a lot of channels that you'll never watch. However, the kid's incessant whining eventually broke us down. Had my kids been German soldiers during World War Two and applied their whining techniques on American G.I.s, them most major U-S cities would end in "burg."

Now that we've taken the cable plunge the kids are ecstatic. They are no longer on the outside looking in. They are on the inside, looking at everything their friends are looking at…or at least they are trying to.

We gave in and got connected.

I have to admit that cable is cool. I have a zillion channels. If I want to watch an old episode of *Get Smart* I can find it. If I want to see Sacramento Kings highlights, they are a remote click away. But the best part about cable television can be summed up in two words—parental control. We are now getting even with the whiners.

My wife and I love that parental control option!

Let's set the scene the day that cable arrived in our home. The kids finally had IT after years of begging. There was a whole New World of programming entertainment at their fingertips. They admired that remote control in their hands. It felt good. Whoever designed the remote got it just right, the way the buttons are within close striking distance of the thumb. When they first caressed that remote they must have truly believed that the guy who designed the thing had kids in mind, otherwise their hand and the remote would not be such a perfect fit.

However, the bliss comes to a painful end when they start cruising through the menu.

"Oooh. It says *The Matrix* is on."

Click. Sorry channel locked.

"Let's check out MTV!"

Click. Sorry, another channel locked.

"Wrestling?!"

Click. Locked.

"What did you do?" they shouted at us. "We can't watch anything!"

"Sure you can," my wife replied. "You can watch anything that doesn't have a little lock next to it on the screen. Anything that has a lock, you need the parental control code, which we'll never tell you. Not if you bribe us. Not even on our deathbeds."

"That's not fair! We finally get cable and we can't watch anything."

Not true. They can watch Nickelodeon, Disney, the Cartoon Network and that crazy crocodile hunter guy who plucks scary snakes from bushes like most of us would snatch up pretty flowers. What they can't watch is Howard Stern, MTV Spring Break Bikini Marathons or Arnold blowing up half of the Earth.

You only have parental control over the kids for so long. Use it while you can. After a while, the whining doesn't bother you any more. It doesn't go away, but it doesn't bother you any more.

MOVIES ARE RATED FOR A REASON!

"Hey, Dad! It's Father's Day. Want to go to the movies?"

My son's invitation touched my heart. He was inviting me to go to the movies. It was an invitation to share some special family time. It was an opportunity to enjoy some bonding time together. But that was just on the surface. Deep down, he was inviting me to take him and the rest of the family to the movies, so that I could squeeze the minivan into a parking spot just right for a mountain bike, pay too much money at the ticket window (unless we hit a matinee or have Entertainment book coupons) and fork over about $37.25 just for the colossal tub of popcorn.

Despite facing the possibility of paying a small fortune for an afternoon of film watching fun, it was a sweet gesture on his part, just the same.

The problem is that we are in a transitional stage in our house when it comes to movies. Our kids range in age from almost twelve-and-a-half to seven-and-a-half. (When you're a kid and you're keeping score on the age thing, those half years are very, very important.) We've reached the point where we either can't agree on what movie to see, or we can't find one that is interesting to the kids, yet age appropriate at the same time.

Whenever we pull out the movie listings to see what's playing at either the Century Laguna or the Laguna UA Theater—two theaters both within a five-minute drive from our home—we run into the same problem that we did the other day.

ME: "How about if we go see that movie about the chickens trying to escape from the farm?"

DAUGHTER (the youngest of four): "YEAH!"

Before you can say "junior mints" she already has her shoes on, her hair brushed back into a tight ponytail and she's ready to go.

But then the older two boys chime in.

BOYS: "No, Dad! That movie is for little kids. Let's go see *Shaft*. That one looks really cool!"

Whoa! Hang on! With all due respect to one of my favorite actors, Samuel L. Jackson, I really don't think my young kids should see that film.

"Guys, that movie is rated 'R'! None of you are old enough to go see it and you won't! Can you dig it?"

Then they got blank stares on their faces. They didn't understand the Shaft humor.

When we get onto the subject of movies and the age appropriate nature of certain films, the kids usually respond: "But our friends are going to see it!"

The truth is, some of their friends WILL see *Shaft* despite the fact that the movie is rated "R." Some parents will let their kids see whatever movies they want without considering the subject matter of the film or the rating.

Films have ratings for a reason. Actually, there are two reasons. Movies are rated so that parents know what is suitable for their kids to see. They are also rated so that kids can learn what films they shouldn't see so that they can work like crazy to see them any way.

So, folks—for anyone who's interested—here are the movie ratings:

G—General audiences. All Ages admitted.

PG—Parental guidance suggested. Some matter may not be suitable for children.

PG-13—Parents strongly cautioned. Some material may be inappropriate for children under 13.

R—Restricted. Under 17 requires accompanying parent or adult guardian.

NC-17—No one under 17 admitted.

And I'd like to add one more: **NWWYSTO**. It stands for "NO WAY WILL YOU SEE THAT ONE!"

It's sad to say that there aren't many good family movies out there any more. Kids still manage to get into theaters to watch movies they're not supposed to see. But I really believe parents need to pay attention to those movie ratings, because it's in the best interest of the children.

I'd like to go see *Shaft*. However, I plan on taking my wife and not my children. Movies are rated for a reason. In the immortal words of John Shaft: "Can you dig it?"

LIKE THE RESULTS OR NOT KIDS LEARNED SOMETHING FROM THE ELECTION

My kids were glued to the television set. The constantly changing score mesmerized them. They cheered. They booed. They gnawed on their fingernails. Crowds of people screamed on TV. Commentators provided constant analysis to accompany the action. My kids have never seen anything like it.

Now they can hardly wait until the 2004 presidential election.

You thought that maybe I was referring to an action packed NBA game. Well, that's what my kids said it was like for them as they watched the election returns coming in on that evening in November 2000.

"Dad, it was like watching a Kings game!" my youngest son, a nine-year-old, said. The political bug bit him the hardest of all my children. The last time he had that much interest in something on the screen, the Kings were battling the Lakers in the playoffs. My wife nearly had to drag the boy to bed because he couldn't tear himself away from the television.

"Can't we wait for the returns from Montana to come in?"

The youngest boy would have stayed up all night if he could have. One of his favorite pastimes is watching professional basketball players streak up and down the hardwood floor in their bright baggy shorts and stylish sneakers. On that election night, guys in dark business suits and polished wingtips captivated him.

"I'll go to bed in a few minutes! Tim Russert is writing some new Electoral College numbers on his white board!"

All my children have become more politically aware, but my third son is evolving into a political animal. His favorite subject at Barbara Comstock Morse Elementary is math, but that might change now. I think he's going to suggest to the school board that the district adopt a policy requiring fourth graders to take political science. If the school district won't offer the class, maybe my son could start a poli-sci study group for budding political junkies.

I don't want to leave you with the impression that he's not a normal nine-year-old any more. He still loves rolling around on his razor scooter. And when his older brother is practicing the saxophone, he will always find the time to accompany classics like "Jingle Bells" with armpit noises. It's just that now he asks about foreign policy and the Electoral College.

The day of the November 2000 election, he got into a discussion about health care with a little boy down the street. The other child (possibly a future political strategist) was trying to convince my son which candidate had the better position on that issue. Then my son came home and started quizzing my wife and me about which candidate we felt had the better stance on the issue.

"Ummmm? Why don't you go ride your bike for a while and stop worrying about co-payments? That'll give Mommy and me time to research that subject and get back to you."

Please don't get me wrong. I am not complaining about my children's newfound interest in politics. I was usually in the dark about most current affairs when I was young.

When I was a kid, I could have told you who was the President but I am positive I would not have been able to tell you anything more than the man's name and where he lived. I couldn't have named the Governor if my life depended on it. Although I did know that Izzy Steiner was on the local town council only because I played baseball with his son Danny and sometimes Mr. Steiner had to miss games because of meetings.

My parents didn't discuss social science a great deal in our house. And that might be the difference right there. My wife and I talk occasionally about candidates and issues at dinner or in the car and maybe the kids have picked up on that.

Maybe it's good to make kids socially aware when they are younger. That way, when they are of voting age, they can make their own choices at the ballot box, vote their consciences and help explain things to me and my wife so we can make informed decisions.

Yard Sales Send Unusual Birds Flocking To Yard

It's that one thing they ache for, that one particular thing that keeps them searching. They are willing to invest hours and hours to find it and save a paltry nickel in the process. It might be pink baby socks, a low mileage Nordic Track, or a battered toaster. Whatever it is, the yard sale veteran will find it.

Working as a reporter has allowed me to meet all kinds of people. I once met a man who was convinced he was God. Although, I had my doubts since the guy didn't know my name until he asked for a business card. There was the lady who insisted she owned the world's largest collection of Barbies. And what about those Star Trek convention goers? Enough said.

I thought I had met my share of "unique" people, until we held our own garage sale.

In my ongoing effort to be as politically correct as possible, let me say that folks who spend their weekends travelling the yard sale circuit are "a different breed." I am not going to say that they are kooks or just plain weird because that might be considered degrading, so I will use words like "different".

When it came time for us to get a bigger home, we were forced to clean out the old one. We had tons of old dishes, children's clothes and scratched up bicycles that could be of use to someone. So we posted signs. We put an ad in the newspaper and followed the old garage sale adage: "IF YOU HOLD ONE, THEY WILL COME!"

And they did.

Garage sale junkies rise long before dawn, with yellow highlighter in hand to mark the classifieds. The coffee maker is on timer so they can get their caffeine shot before charging into battle. They are bargain hunting, driveway warriors armed with purses full of dimes and quarters.

My wife and I were not sure what to expect from our garage sale, which was scheduled to run from 7:00 AM. until 1:00 PM. Here were the highlights:

5:00 AM—Alarm sounds.

6:00 AM—Start setting up.

6:35 AM—First customer arrives twenty-five minutes early! "Can I just look around?" Sure, we say. She leaves minutes later after spending four-dollars on some nice old clothes while beating those other bargain hunters to the punch.

7:00 AM—We cheerfully greet customers courteous enough to respect the posted start time.

7:20 AM—Dozens of people come and go. We've hauled in about thirty-dollars.

8:00 AM—Crowd starts thinning. Probably checking out competing yard sales. I should have ripped down the other signs the night before.

8:30 AM—Woman snags armload of children's clothing and insists on paying only five-dollars for the whole pile. Plus she wants some toys. We're startled by her pushiness. No, we said. The toys are extra. She scowls but stands firm on the five-dollars for the clothes. We accept, hoping she'll leave. She does. We're five bucks richer and she's gone.

9:00 AM—A mother of five boys, finds clothes for her kids. No negotiations needed. We take whatever she offers because she's a nice lady.

9:30 AM—Potential customers slow down and speed off in their cars after only a glance. We feel embarrassed by the fact that they won't even stop to browse.

9:30AM to 11:30AM—Customers trickle in and out. Cash flow is steady.

11:30AM—Husband and wife arrive in station wagon. We spend thirty minutes chatting as they peruse our inventory. We talk about their 51-years of marriage, their grandchildren and great grandchildren. Nice old couple spends fifty cents on some little toys before heading off to another garage sale.

1:00 PM—Store closes. We are grateful.

It was a fascinating day, and slightly embarrassing. When you're holding a garage sale, you're selling off little pieces of your past. You want a buck for an item you bought for twenty dollars five years ago, and the buyer laughs and offers a dime. You barter and agree on twenty-cents. And you ask yourself, why am I dickering over nickels when I'm just trying to unload this junk in the first place?

When the day is finally over, the really good stuff is gone. The leftovers are packed away for charity. The shoebox rattles from the change. And you have this premonition that the people who picked through your old stuff will be on someone else's driveway next weekend.

Then when the hectic day is done you look out the window and spot someone driving by slowly, well past the end of your semi-successful yard sale, looking for straggling bargains in the driveway.

They are a different breed, those garage sale people.

There Is No Sanctuary In Yard Work

Just when you think you know who your friends are, they don't really help when you need them the most. I'm talking about people who have the nerve to actually lend you tools to take on tough jobs you don't want to do.

Last weekend was our first fairly warm and dry period in ages. The nice weather meant opportunity to me. It meant the NCAA basketball playoffs are on television and I can enjoy a bag of Ruffles and, at the same time, bask in the sunshine coming in through the window thus avoiding exposure to potentially harmful ultraviolet rays.

But it meant something else to my wife. In her eyes, it was a perfect time to toil under the warm sun, dethatch the front lawn and cut down that dead bush that's been a potential fire hazard since the summer.

I tried to handle the situation with solid reasoning, but my wife never understands such guy type of logic concerning general laziness. I tried convincing her that it was more than a privilege, it was a right to lay on the couch and gorge myself with salty, unhealthy food products and watch sports on television. Needless to say, her definition of weekend activity won out and for that reason my muscles still ache today. I really shouldn't blame my wife. She just wants things to look nice. So maybe in this instance the one I really should be blaming is a neighbor that we'll call "Mike"…because…well…that's his name.

"Mike" owns more yard tools than I do. Actually, most people in North America and in some desert nations own more yard tools than I do. It's part of my overall plan. The fewer tools you own, the better chance you have at avoiding certain types of yard work.

"Let's cut back this tree," my wife will say. And I respond: "Well, I really should use a tree saw for that, but unfortunately I don't have one."

You can't do the work if you lack the proper equipment. That's just how my system has worked over the years…until this past weekend…when my wife said: "Well, let's see if 'Mike' has any tools we can use!"

I was dead meat.

Of course, "Mike" had an axe. And of course, "Mike" has an electric hedge trimmer. So, of course, that meant I was forced into doing the bothersome yard jobs I had been skirting for many weeks, even months I am proud to say.

I spent about twenty hours on Sunday raking, chopping, whacking and cursing. My wife insists it was more like three hours, because she out there for much of the time too. I scraped a ton of dead grass from my lawn. I destroyed the fire hazard bush and most of its four-mile root system. I missed the college basketball games. And I think that maybe I should be in traction right now. Even my whining is giving me a muscle cramp.

After I was finished destroying nature with the tools "Mike" had loaned to us, I hosed the thick layers of mud off of them and carted them back to his house.

I think he took one look at me and was shrouded with guilt…guilt for having made those blasted garden tools available…guilt for not realizing he should have helped me preserve my nearly foolproof system of yard work avoidance.

"Honey," he yelled to his wife, "Do you think we could provide Tim with sanctuary here? Maybe political asylum?"

"No. We'd better not," she shouted back. "There might be more yard work for him to do."

I schlepped my way back home, having felt the letdown of not gaining amnesty in my neighbor's home and having had a lengthy yard work avoidance streak broken.

In retrospect, "Mike" did the right thing. When I got home, I realized that the yard did look better kept. The huge pile of dead grass served as the mark of a true accomplishment. But my arms and my back were throbbing, and that negated any feelings of achievement that I had gained.

The bottom line is this: I gotta get some good yard tools. That way I can either avoid all the effort of avoiding the work, or perhaps some day lend those tools to some poor slob like me who thought he had his weekend all figured out.

FAITH

"Trust yourself. You know more than you think you do."

Dr. Benjamin Spock, American
Pediatrician, address to new parents

"Before God we are all equally wise—and equally foolish."

Albert Einstein

TEACHER, HOW COME I WASN'T JESUS?

Kids say the darndest things. No, wait. That's an overused phrase.

How about: kids say the cutest things. No. That's not going to apply here.

How about: kids sometimes ask incredibly complex questions that cause adults to squirm and that complexity multiplies when it's other peoples' kids who are doing the asking.

That's closer to the point I'm trying to make.

Our children have all taken turns asking some extremely difficult questions. My wife and I have sometimes stretched the truth to provide easy answers. Well, actually my wife always gives the best answer possible. I often take the easy way out and offer up an occasional "ask your mother" type of response, or avoid the truth all together.

"Daddy, why is the sky blue?"

"Because the color green was already taken by the grass, sweetheart."

When it's your own child, you can skate around the truth, until you can figure out the right answer. However, when it's someone else's child doing the asking, it is a different ballgame.

My wife agreed to be a religious education teacher this year. Good Shepherd Church needed help teaching the children of our parish and my wife—as she often does—volunteered. If people ask for assistance, whether it's with school or church, my wife finds a way to squeeze a few more hours out of her week to help. On the other hand, I manage to squirm out of volunteering opportunities. That's what makes us the perfect couple.

My wife usually assisted with religious education classes in the past, but this time she decided to take on the big job. She thought, fourth grade religion class…they'll talk about being kind to your neighbor, treating people like you want to be treated and kneeling and standing at the right times during mass. How hard could it be? But always remember; never ask how hard could it be. You might just find out.

The class has ten students. My nine-year-old son is among them. The kids come to our house for an hour each week. They sit on the floor and discuss their lessons. Or at least, that's the way it's supposed to be. It seems the curious kids are conjuring up lessons of their own and my wife finds herself scrambling for the right answers to their questions.

The other day, the kids started asking about Jesus. Seems like a good topic of discussion for a group of fourth graders, right? Well?

Things went smoothly until the kids lined up like a firing squad and blasted away with some involved questions.

"How did Jesus get to be Jesus? Wasn't there anybody else who wanted to be him?"

"Yeah…how come I couldn't be Jesus?"

"How did Jesus get in Mary's belly?"

My wife is a trained teacher. She knows how to handle a classroom full of inquisitive kids, but she is not a theologian. She answered the questions as best she could—between wiping beads of sweat from her brow—while trying to move along with the lesson.

By the time the parents came, picked up their children and rescued my wife, her head was spinning. I laughed when she repeated their tough questions but she didn't see as much humor in the situation as I did. Of course, I could laugh. I wasn't the one getting grilled with all the Jesus questions.

So, the weekend after my wife's inquisition, she cornered our pastor, Father Philip Wells, and replayed the entire ordeal for him. He smiled occasionally and laughed a few times, and even raised his eyebrows at some of the kids' questions.

"The kids in your class are at an age where they are very inquisitive," Father Wells said as he smiled. Then he advised my wife on how to handle some of the real toughies in regards to Jesus and subjects like heaven and hell. Father also suggested that she set aside a few minutes in each class for questions that did not pertain to the lesson, but to remind the young interrogators that they need to stay on task. And the best thing he told her was that if she felt uncomfortable with any of the questions, that she should refer the inquiring children to him.

Kids do ask the darndest questions. And it's nice to know that if you don't have the answers, you can always say "ask your pastor."

SANTA'S GOT A BRAND NEW BAG

This Christmas is going to be different in a sad sort of way. I thought I had a few more years to relish the magic. Now I'm going to miss it for what it was and will have to learn to appreciate it for what it is.

Let me speak as cryptically as possible here. Without giving too much detail, the cat is out of the bag in regards to the plump and jolly North Pole guy. The youngest of my four kids is now wise to Kris Kringle, his reindeer, the chimney thing and the mystery that surrounds Christmas.

It makes me sad when I should be happy.

Our boys caught on some time ago and kept quiet, mainly because of threats of physical harm and economic sanctions. There are stiff penalties for uncovering THAT kind of truth to younger siblings before the time is right. As my daughter was turning eight years old, she was the last hold-out. I was clinging to the hope that her wide-eyed view of Christmas would survive for another year. Just one more year.

I knew time was running out because she is in that age group when young girls are crazy about the face glitter and the hair done just so and they debate long into the night of a sleepover as to which Backstreet Boy is the cutest.

There's a period of silence and then an outburst of giggling, which is followed by more silence and then more giggling. What's that all about?

I wasn't ready for her to grow up. I wanted one more holiday season steeped in puzzles of where the presents come from, how they get there and who ate all of the cookies yet failed to drink the milk. But a few weeks before Saint Nick's annual hernia producing pilgrimage to our house, my daughter was riding in the minivan with just me and my wife, and she confided in us what she knew and I felt my heart shatter into a million pieces.

"Mom, Dad, is there really a Santa Claus?"

A dagger to my heart! She went from my sweetheart baby girl, sitting on my lap listening to Dr. Seuss to a young woman ready for a briefing on her 401K plan.

And it didn't stop with the one question. She kept firing them at us. Her every query was like a punch to the stomach, each one knocking the wind out of me. The old saying "the truth hurts" was certainly true that day.

"Yes, you're right sweetie," my wife confessed. "You've figured it out, but let me tell you why…"

My wife is a kindergarten teacher and a much better explainer of the ways of the world that I am. She went into great detail about the history of Saint Nicholas and the folklore regarding the elves and how it's not that parents are tricking their children to make them feel foolish, but that it all has to do with the spirit of giving.

My daughter grinned, pleased for figuring out the mystery herself. I wasn't smiling though. I was disappointed. The fun was supposed to last a little longer. All I wanted was one more year with reindeer on the roof and one last pile of presents from the man in the red suit who knows who's been bad or good.

Now I'm going to miss staying up all night, skinning my knuckles while putting toys together until my fingers are numb and I can no longer see straight. I'm going to miss that satisfying feeling that comes from finishing all the assembling, creeping up the stairs, tired and exhausted, peeking in all the bedrooms to make sure the little ones were asleep through all the clatter downstairs. Gifts with "some assembly required" can now wait until morning.

We've moved on to another phase. My wife and I will still be sneaking gifts into the house. We'll still leave surprises wrapped under the tree. But now that my youngest—the last holdout—knows the source of all the spoils, things won't be the same.

Actually, Christmases will still be great because all the necessary ingredients are still there. As I am writing this, my wife is in the kitchen whipping up her world famous coffeecakes, which we give as presents. That makes the house smell like Christmas morning. My boys are battling over who gets to lick the tasty, gooey batter from the mixing spoons. And my wise-for-her-age daughter—the last holiday magic holdout—keeps running by the Christmas tree and rearranging the wrapped gifts she's hand made for all of us. She's still excited about the holiday, mystery solved or not.

But the thing I will miss the most is that initial, ecstatic gasp the little ones give out when they discover all that surprise stuff under the tree. Nothing compares to the radiant face of a young child whose wishes come true on Christmas morning thanks to the hard work of a saintly, generous guy who works his tail off for one special night each year.

I must say, it was a blast while it lasted.

FINDING FAITH WHEN IT'S MISSING

"I'm really scared," my youngest son's voice quivers. "I've been thinking about it all day. It's scary!"

We are thousands of miles away from ground zero of our nation's worst catastrophe, and even farther away from the retaliation being waged on foreign soil, yet my ten-year-old son living in seemingly safe suburbia is frightened. He wants to know could it happen around here? Could someone blast big buildings nearby and kill a lot of people?

How do you answer that truthfully? How do you tell your kids that while the world seems to be falling apart that they need to have faith that everything will be okay?

"It's not easy but we have to believe that things will turn out all right. Unfortunately, a lot of countries hate America," I say while placing the napkins around the dinner table. "A lot of countries want to destroy us."

"Why?" they ask. It is a one-word question asked at the dinner table that requires an infinite number of words that don't really supply a sufficient answer.

It seems as if it has been so long since the initial attacks and we still have knots in our stomachs. The knots are permanent. The images are indelible. The heartache we feel burns white hot. Our anger boils. A tall masterpiece of ingenuity in America's biggest city crumbles into a mammoth heap of smoking debris. Thousands of people were murdered simply because they are Americans who were in the wrong place at the wrong time. Try explaining that to your kids. Try telling them that they have to rely on faith that everything will be fine when your own faith has been shaken.

Everywhere, people are crying. Children lost their parents. Wives lost their husbands. Firefighters and police officers lost close friends.

Thousands of miles away, we grieve for people that we've never met and now never will.

For many Americans, it's difficult to imagine living in a country where the threat of that level of violence is so genuine. We are used to the good and safe life. We are used to dropping off our children at school, pulling into Starbucks for a latte and then briskly merging onto a crowded highway for our commute to the office. Grab a CD and pop it in the player. Check the gas gauge to make sure there's enough $1.75-a-gallon fuel to last for a while. While we're behind the wheel, we're thinking about how to get our kid's to soccer practice on time, what drive-through to hit for dinner on the way home and what movie to pick up at Blockbuster for the night's entertainment.

We are not thinking about savage lawlessness, especially on our own soil, especially in New York City or at the Pentagon. Why should we? This is America. This is where you do your fifty hard hours a week to earn a good living to buy a nice house and pay for dance lessons and braces for your kids teeth. This is where you dial 911 and the cops come. This is where you have a choice between the fresh produce at Bel Air or Costco or Safeway. This is where you can walk out of Sunday morning mass and strike up a conversation at a local coffee shop with a good friend and ask them how things are at their synagogue.

Now this is also a place where you have to worry, or at least think about terrorism. Terrorism, anarchy or whatever you want to call it is very real now. Now we have to explain that to our children. Now it's part of their lives and will be a part of their memories of childhood. What they may remember more than the sad images on television is the seriousness in their parents' tone, the way they talk and act. The tension, that's what the kids will remember.

I remember watching television reports about the Vietnam War when I was a kid. It looked scary, but I didn't think about it too much. Vietnam was far from Pittsburgh and I was just a kid. That all changed when my father got a phone call in the middle of the night telling him that my second cousin, Jimmie from Detroit, was shot down during a mission. Jimmie was a gunner. He manned machine guns inside helicopters that flew dangerous missions. Our family always hoped and prayed that he would return home safely, his father would hug him and he'd settle into a normal life.

Obviously, our prayers were not answered.

My father took the train to Detroit to attend the funeral. I wanted to go with him. He said no. Instead, the rest of us stayed home and prayed for Jimmie, his brothers and sisters and his parents.

Now we continue to pray for these people in New York and in D.C. and for their families. We have to pray that our country finds a way to keep this type of thing from happening again so that little children—like ones living in places like Elk Grove, California—don't have to ask "why" questions that are so hard to answer.

We have to find faith and hope that faith finds out children.

FAMILY

"Many parents are so influenced by psychological theories about child rearing that they disregard common sense."

P. Dalton

"Having a family is like having a bowling alley installed in your brain."

Martin Mull, Actor/Artist

THE SHORT TRIP THAT WENT A LONG WAY

It's not very often that my wife and I are the envy of our friends.

When we bought a new minivan a few years ago, several of our closest friends were complimentary and congratulatory, but they were not envious. Our van did have power windows, removable seats and a CD player, but all that's standard equipment these days. Our friends yawned at those features.

A few months ago, we bought a new house. You'd think that would make others jealous, but it didn't. People visited and appreciated the "new" smell of the place. They made glowing remarks about our platinum taupe carpet, our white window dressings and our landscaped backyard. But most of our friends moved into new homes shortly before we did, so our housing adventure was nothing special to them.

But a few weeks ago, something happened that had several of our friends blurt out comments like: "You two are so lucky!" or "We wish we could do that!" or "We totally hate your guts and are severing this friendship." Okay, I made up that last one.

We didn't win any money from Regis Philbin. We didn't qualify for a new reality program like "SURVIVOR...AT THE MALL AFTER THE FOOD COURT CLOSES!" No, we did something we haven't done for years...we had a few days away without the kids!

(Insert applause and cheering noises here. If you are throwing confetti, please pick it up yourselves. Don't get any on my new platinum taupe carpet!)

My in-laws were coming from Pennsylvania for the annual visit that they intentionally make every few years or so and they offered to stay with our four children so that we could get away and have some time alone. They made the offer weeks before they arrived. My wife and I mulled over our decision for about a nanosecond, made hotel reservations in Lake Tahoe and had a bag packed and ready long before my in-laws were boarding their plane for the West Coast.

When the grandparents arrived, we anxiously greeted them, chatted and spent a few days catching up. Yeah, yeah, come on, come on. Sure we're interested in Aunt Gertie's gout. Yes, those slides taken during your wart removal are incredibly graphic and colorful. Of course, we want to hear about how today's slothful kids don't appreciate what the hard working people of past generations have done for them. But when can we leave? Here are directions to nearby stores, parks and movie theaters. Here's a list of what the kids will eat and won't eat. If they fight, turn the garden hose on them. Here's a phone number where we can be reached. See ya. Bye! Then we raced out the door before my wife's parents changed their minds.

(Insert sound of squealing tires here.)

To sum up our short trip: it was a blast. We stayed in a nice hotel. We spent some time in the casinos watching people—many of whom looked like they didn't have two nickels to rub together—give buckets full of money back to "the house." On the other hand, my wife and I had a gaming plan. Play with fifty bucks. When it's gone, it's gone. And it went, fairly quickly. We played games with nickels, dimes and quarters, lost it all and enjoyed every minute of it. We went out to dinner and had hours of uninterrupted adult conversation. We didn't have to cut up anyone's meat or tell anyone to stop standing on his or her chair. However, that one guy getting ready to dance on the table could have used a few harsh words and a stern fatherly look to calm him down. The bicycle ride along the lake was soothing and breathtaking at the same time.

The best part was that we got to spend some time alone together. That's something that we don't do nearly enough. I don't know many married couples with kids that do get away often enough.

This is not a knock against our children. We passionately love them with all our hearts and would do anything for them and prove it by our selfless actions time and again. But sometimes the busy-ness associated with raising children slows the growth of a loving relationship. Now and then, parents have to take a time out to get reacquainted and reconnected with each other.

We returned home refreshed, relaxed and content. Our kids survived our time away. So did their grandparents. Now my wife and I have to work on getting Grandma and Grandpa back for another visit. We're looking forward to making our friends envious again.

MOM'S STORIES

My wife's intentions are always good. The kids know that. But there are times when the kids want to stay very far away from their Mom's good intentions. When my wife has her good intentions on the tarmac and ready for takeoff, the kids would rather be hiding out in Canada, wearing fake beards, using assumed names and finishing every sentence with "Eh!" My wife's stories have that kind of exaggerated affect on the children…at least for now. We're hoping that they'll come to appreciate her personal tales later in their lives.

It all starts innocently enough. We'll be sitting around the dinner table when one of the children pipes up about a problem at school and before they realize it they have been sucked inescapably into another episode of "Mom's Meaningful Stories."

"There's this one kid who keeps messing around in math class and getting me in trouble," one of our four children will moan. "I don't know what to do about it."

Then there is an eerie silence hanging over the dinner table like a dark cloud, or the smoke from an overcooked meatloaf. The children pause in mid-chew. Their eyes widen. They jerk their heads back and forth at each other in desperation. And before they can blurt out a blood curdling "OH NO!"…my wife begins a monologue with the words…"I remember once when…"

Then the children drop their heads in disgust, furious with themselves for walking right into the story trap. They look like deer caught in the headlights. They are trapped. There is no escape.

"When I was in school there was this one kid named…" my wife will continue. She is fully aware of the kid's overwhelming desire to escape the dinner table, even if it means missing dessert but they are obligated to stay.

Not listening to one of their mother's anecdotes is not an option. The children no longer feign emergency trips to the bathroom, spontaneous urges to finish math homework or sudden desires to pick up dirty clothes from beneath, beside and on top of their beds. It has taken years to enlighten them but they are now trained to listen. Even though the odds are that they have heard the story of the moment several times before and will no doubt hear it again—and again—they listen. They listen out of respect for their mother and out fear of reprisal.

They also have learned that these stories contain important messages. When my wife begins to tell a story, it's like listening to one of Aesop's Fables. There is a beginning, middle and an end. And there is always a moral to the story.

One of the most often recurring stories is the one about the time she didn't make the cheerleading squad when all of her friends did. This heart-tugging tale involves a young girl's excitement, hard work and her pitiful disappointment when she got lost in the middle of her audition. The rest—as the saying goes—is cheerleading history.

That specific story is reserved for times when the children need a lesson in dealing with disappointments in life.

Another one of her favorites involves a young man named Lenny Zarmack. She went to elementary school with him. He is now in his forties and is no doubt living his life totally unaware of the fact that his is still the focus of one of my wife's choice narratives.

You see, Lenny and my wife were once sweethearts. I accept this. And I am not the least bit jealous. I am now in my mid-forties, have been married for nearly eighteen years and am somewhat confident in the thought that my wife does not dream of running off with Lenny and leaving me with our four children. She might consider running off with Tom Cruise or Richard Gere, but I think Lenny is several slots down on the list.

Any way, for a Valentine's Day many, many years ago, a young Lenny presented my (future) wife with a card that he made out of construction paper and ribbons. She kept that special card for years and years and years.

In fact, she didn't get rid of it until shortly before we got married. She thought that I would be upset about it…that I would become enraged over the fact that she was still clinging onto a homemade Valentine's Day card made by a former beau from decades before. How silly! How could I get upset over something like that? However if the stupid, stupid card were to have accidentally disappeared and ended up in a New Jersey land-fill or served to ignite a pile of fireplace kindling, that would not have been my fault. Why? Because I am a very secure man. Yes. Very secure. You bet. Secure for sure.

Any way, that extraordinary card touched her heart. In fact, it meant so much to her that to this day, she talks about how those kinds of gifts from the heart are the types of gifts that mean the most to people.

Our kids are just beginning to enter the teenage years. What they do no know is that my wife has a huge reserve of life's stories stashed away inside her mind. They are categorized and cross-referenced and ready for just the proper occasion. My wife has many more stories that do not involve cheer-leading or Lenny Zarmack, but do involve disappointment, missed oppor-tunities and making the right choices. And when the time comes for the children to hear these other stories they will moan and groan as their mother launches into another monologue, but they will listen and they will learn.

Somehow I think they know that stories with good morals stand the test of time.

NEW FURNITURE

When I was a kid, it was a big deal when someone in the neighborhood got new furniture. It was an event. Sometimes it was a bigger deal than getting a new car. I never understood.

"Margie and Ralph, you and the kids gotta come over," one of the neighbors would tell my folks. "We got this new couch. You oughta see it with lime green shag carpeting! We thought it would clash but it don't."

We'd process over to the proud neighbor's house and behold their new sofa on display, or sort of on display. It was often hidden underneath a blanket, or covered with doilies or that clear plastic covering that made your bum sweat, even in the wintertime. We knew there was a couch under there somewhere. Our neighbors wouldn't lie about something that serious. We always accepted their claim on good faith.

My folks would touch the couch, almost like petting a soft, exotic animal. They'd "ooh" and "ah" over it. It was like a ritual to fuss over new home furnishings, as if purchasing them were a grand accomplishment.

I never understood why a piece of furniture was such a big deal. After all, a couch was just a couch. It was something to leap from like a high dive, or spring over like a hurdle or splatter with chocolate milk while laughing hysterically at the Three Stooges.

But now I know why a new couch is such a big deal. It took forty-two years to reach this level of enlightenment.

Just before we moved into our new house, my wife laid down the law.

"THAT RATTY OLD COUCH AND LOVE SEAT WILL NOT COME WITH US!"

We'd had the set since we first got married. When we bought the matching loveseat and couch with a fold out bed, it was a cool beige corduroy, like so many other furniture sets from the 80s. Fifteen years later, it evolved into a battered, beaten, lumpy yet still strangely comfortable duo. But sadly, the stuff had to go. We'd tried getting rid of the junk…I mean, well worn and well cared for furnishings several times before, without luck. We'd tried selling the stuff. We tried giving it away. We put it on the curb with a "FREE COUCH AND LOVE SEAT" sign and there were never any takers.

Then we had a garage sale and the furniture Gods smile upon us. The beige beast and it's little buddy sidekick sat on the sidewalk with a sign that read: "FOR SALE $50." In the waning minutes of our yard sale, the matching corduroy set remained available. My wife was willing to saturate the stuff in gasoline and torch the junk right there. Fortunately, we were able to avoid creating a bonfire when a young man came up and asked: "Do you want $50 for the couch and loveseat?" "Oh, no," I answered. "How about $30." We shook hands. He handed over the cash. A friend of mine came by with his pickup truck and we helped take it to the buyer's house. Home delivery? I would have carried that furniture to San Francisco on my back to get rid of it.

The buyer seemed anxious to get the furniture and grateful for the help in transporting the junk…I mean, well worn home furnishings. His home was only a few miles from mine, but by the time we backed the pickup into the man's driveway it made me feel as if we lived worlds apart.

Boards covered most of the windows of the home suffering from dry rot and a complete lack of attention. One side of the garage door was higher than the other side. A broken spring protruding out the front appeared to be the culprit. The lawn was a sea of waist high weeds and crabgrass, littered with discarded aluminum cans and dog droppings. But one glance around the neighborhood proved that this home was in better condition that most of the others. I imagined that the ratty furniture we delivered to this grateful man's home might have been the finest furnishing he now owned. If I hadn't already handed the $30 to my wife before we left to make this eye-opening delivery, I would have handed the money back.

Now we own a brand new couch and it's the biggest thing I've ever seen. It's a puffy, hunter green sectional—complete with recliner—that wraps around the corner of the family room. It's massive and it's comfortable and it's not lumpy. Now I know why my parents and their friends made such a big deal out of buying new furniture. It does provide a feeling of accomplishment, in a way.

Now, we have a new set of house rules. No one can eat while sitting on the new couch. There will be no jumping on the new couch. And there will definitely be no leaping on, hurdling over or chocolate milk drinking anywhere near the new couch.

Now, we have to start inviting the neighbors over to look at the great green Titanic of furniture. And those neighbors will bring their children, who will no doubt look at a brand new couch and see a trampoline.

For the guy who bought our old couch and loveseat, I hope the stuff is holding up well. And I hope that, some day, if you are ever in a position to pass the beige beasts on to someone else, that you show more charity than I did to help you avoid the feelings of regret that come from not doing someone a good turn just because it was the right thing to do.

Pitching In To Help The Family Survive And Save

In a busy household as large as ours, everyone has chores. Or at least they're supposed to have chores. Put two adults and four children under one roof and you'll find a constant state of chaos unless people pitch in. Whether they are assigned or self-appointed to each family member, certain jobs must be done to insure that things run smoothly inside the home.

My wife and I do most of the work. Okay, my wife does most of the work, but we've always told our children that they must also do their parts to help out. We tell them that it's just a part of life.

For instance, my seven-year-old daughter has one main chore assigned to her, keeping her room clean enough to avoid health department inspections. She rarely completes this task without constant badgering from my wife and me. But when she does finish this chore, it's nice to be reminded that my little girl does have carpeting on her bedroom floor.

Her self appointed chore would best be titled "Instigator of All Petty Arguments That Almost Result in Physical Violence Among Siblings." We're trying to think of a shorter title in case she wants to add this talent to her resume or on business cards some day.

My one son, in addition to keeping his bedroom clean and dusting when asked also has a self-assigned duty. The title would be described this way: "Collector of Massive Amounts of Dirty Clothing Beneath the Bed." For the record, he does lug his dirty duds to the laundry room, but it would be an easier job for him if only we would allow him to operate a forklift.

My wife does the cooking, the majority of the cleaning, money managing, the laundry and all other motherly duties that fall under the title. Her self-assigned job would be best described as "The Household Conscience." She is the one who reminds ALL OF US of the "right things to do" during certain situations. She also has a remarkable accuracy rate on that subject matter of about 99.999%, which is really annoying at times.

My jobs include yard work (expect for flower planting which is done by my wife), barbecuing, cleaning the kitchen after meals, unclogging toilets and providing semi-inspirational speeches following disappointing subpar athletic performances by the kids.

Over the years, my one self-assigned responsibility has involved roaming around the house, after all the kids have left for school or gone out to play, in search of lights left burning and non-essential electrical appliances turned on. That would make me the "Electricity Saver Guy."

My children have the ability to storm the house all at once and flip on every light switch, television, fan and stereo within seconds. Walk into the garage, and the lights are on. Enter a closet and the overheard light is burning. An unwatched television is blaring in one room, competing with a stereo that's playing music for no one.

This bugs me to no end! I keep telling the kids that their habits are costing us money, but they fail to make the connection between a burning lightbulb and money.

Mario Moreno is a guy who lives not too far from us and works as an Energy Specialist for SMUD, the Sacramento Municipal Utility District, and the source of our juice. He told me that it's important to teach kids at an early age the importance of saving energy.

"The earlier you start, the more ahead you are in the game," Moreno said. "It plays a big part in your (energy saving) habits and it starts at an early age."

Mario advised that parents should equate turning off unneeded lights and appliances to saving aluminum cans—eventually you'll see some savings! Mario said a 60-watt lightbulb would have to run around sixteen hours to use ten cents worth of electricity. "And that ten-cents can add up really quickly," Mario said.

So, from now on my new self-assigned duty to go along with being "Electricity Saver Guy" will be "Savings Reminder Man." If I can convince my kids that turning off every light and television when not in use is like saving money for a Dairy Queen peanut buster parfait or a video game rental, then maybe the lightbulbs will go on in their heads.

Some Dinner Conversations Are Not For Weak Stomachs

"How was school today?"

"How did practice go?"

"Any idea who broke that chair?"

There was a time when my wife and I looked forward to dinner and the dinner table discussions with our children. We regarded it as a precious time to catch up on each other's lives. We'd beg our kids to use napkins instead of their sleeves, then we'd ask a few questions. Simple questions to find out simple pieces of information like what they're up to, what their hopes and dreams are, who they're hanging out with and if any of their buddies are…I don't know…breaking into ATMs or boosting cars.

During our dinner conversations after very busy days, we'd unsuccessfully try to convince our four kids of the benefits of green, leafy vegetables, then we'd talk some more.

"Who wants to watch that millionaire game show tonight and make fun of the geeky contestants?"

That's the way things used to be way back when the kids were pure and clean little guys. Now it seems that the innocence is gone. My wife and I once looked forward to sitting down to supper and catching up with the kids. We'd dish out apple sauce and pour glasses of milk and try to spend each moment as most parents should…intensely interrogating their kids to see what they've been up to. Not any more. Now we look more forward to the end of the meal when the kids are away from the table and we have a few moments of peace.

When it comes to dinner table dialogue, we've reached a new height…or depth in this matter.

The kids used to say things like: "Guess what happened at school today?" or "Did you see the drawing I made for you?"

Now its: "Guess who puked at lunch today?"…And…"This one dude at school had this gigantic thing sticking out of his nose and then he…" And before you know it, we are racing down a path of conversation that is not meant to be heard by people who are eating or by those with weak stomachs.

Grossness—I am told—is the by-product of a family unit composed mostly of young boys. I only have an older sister. While growing up, we never broached the same discussion topics that are the favorites of my kids. My sister never took a liking to coarse subjects. I wasn't very successful at getting the ball rolling down the road to grossness since I worked alone as a kid. But now I have three sons and there is strength in numbers. So, during dinner the unrefined boys wrestle away control of the conversation and steer it toward the ill-mannered side of life to which they have become so very skilled.

I won't gag you with all the dialogue details. Suffice it to say that most of the verbal exchanges in our home involve smelly things, things that ooze, numerous forms of regurgitation and socially unacceptable noises made by various body parts. The boys are even so creative that they have written catchy tunes about disgusting maladies that can be cleared up with over the counter medications…the pink kind.

On the flip side, when my wife and I are caught in a moment of weakness, we do laugh. When my mother was visiting during the kids' Thanksgiving vacation, she laughed until she cried. Unfortunately, this just encourages them and gives them greater momentum. The horses are already galloping out of the barn and my wife and I are laughing too hard to bother to close the door.

As parents, we are searching for a resolution. And we think our best option is to do what any responsible couple would do. We're thinking we should capitalize on the situation and make some money off this whole thing. Tune into almost any situation comedy on television and you'll hear the same detestable, juvenile dialogue. The jokes are sophomoric. The characters are childlike, especially the adults. And the situations often revolve around revolting matters. So, maybe I can see about getting my boys jobs as comedy writers for some network, or maybe one of those cable television outlets that seem to have an endless supply of stupid shows. My kids can be just as creative as the folks banging out some of today's "cutting edge comedy."

Unfortunately, there is money to be made from being gross. But let's not talk about this over dinner.

Sweaters Times Infinity

If you absolutely hate Christmas shopping, take pleasure in knowing that you don't have much time left. No matter what time of the year it is right now, in regards to Christmas shopping…YOU ARE RUNNING OUT OF TIME! It always seems as if we just finished raking up the shredded merry wrapping paper from the family room floor before we have to start planning our last minute shopping frenzy for the next year.

Personally, I think buying presents for children is easy these days.

What do you get for the kid who has everything?

More of everything else, naturally.

You just check out the latest hot cartoon program or live action show and then go in search of the related action figure or video game at your nearest Target or Wal-Mart. Of course, that effort is typically followed by the clerk laughing in your face because the store ran out—in early November—of "that thing every other kid is going to have."

Then, after you've gotten over the humiliation of having some 17-year-old pimple faced kid berate you, you tell yourself next year will be different. But the haunting laughter of the smug young clerk ringing in your ears tells you differently.

I think buying presents for adults—especially parents—is more difficult these days. Thanks to my lack of creative gift ideas, my mother has enough sweaters and bath oils to last forever. In fact, if she took one bath a day with the oils we've given her, she would have to live to the ripe—yet prune skinned—old age of 137 to use up all of that stuff. She'll never be able to finish all the books I've sent her. She could start her own bookstore and sell off her healthy inventory over the course of a few years before we would have to restock the shelves.

So, what do you get for the Mom who has everything? She has enough sweaters. She has sweaters times infinity!

She's probably the only 77-year-old in her hometown that could keep a pair of slippers in every room of the house if she wanted. And over the years, I've started to run dry of ideas. Now, if toy manufacturers made "Diagnosis Murder" and "Touched by an Angel" action figures, I'd be set for a while. But since I can't find a Dick Van Dyke doll with karate chop action, I'm out of luck on the action figure front.

What can you possibly get for the Mom who really doesn't need anything?

That's always been a tough one. But one Christmas my older sister came up with a great role reversal kind of a gift idea. She thought we should get Mom a puppy for Christmas. At the time, Dad had been gone almost seven years and Mom had been living alone. My sister and I moved away years before, so the old house was pretty empty. The house was fairly quiet, except for the blaring TV or the occasional visiting neighbor coming by to chat. So, we thought a pet, a companion, would be a good gift.

We decided not to make it a surprise gift. We asked Mom ahead of time. You don't give a puppy to anyone—especially your Mom—without asking first. We fully expected to make a long sales pitch and use words like "companionship" and "loneliness" but we were shocked when Mom said "yes" so quickly. She was far away from family—or should I say family was far away from her—and was tired of being alone. It was time for Mom to get a housemate…and what better housemate than a young dog that has not yet graduated from House Training School.

Her new friend became a little guy named Rascal, a gray and white schnauzer. My sister and I hoped he'd be exactly what Mom needed to keep her busy and keep her company. Mom hooked up with Rascal weeks before that Christmas so that they could get used to each other. "So how are you and Rascal getting along?" I'd ask. And Mom said things like: "He sure has a lot of energy." And that translated to mean: "The mongrel has knocked over all of my lamps!" She also told me: "He's a very busy dog."

That's another phrase for: "He's hidden my glasses and chewed up my TV GUIDE, so now I don't know when 'Murder She Wrote' is on!"

It took a few months for Mom and her high energy, four-legged, slobbering pal to get used to each other. The little guy has gotten over baseboard gnawing and newspaper shredding. Mom seems to have gotten over those destructive personality traits in exchange for a devoted companion that sits on her lap in perfect petting position. Good friends can be very forgiving.

REMEMBERING TO PROPERLY REMEMBER YOUR MOTHER

The colorful bouquet of cardboard flowers, planted in a blue, plastic Dixie cup was just the right touch. It helped set the Mother's Day breakfast mood. My wife sat at the table, admiring the hand-made gifts from our four children, while she politely worked her way through her lukewarm egg and cheese burrito, her side order of crispy microwaved bacon and a fairly recently unwrapped poppy seed muffin from Safeway.

Another Mother's Day came and went and, once again, we did our best to give that important day the hoopla it deserves in our house. My wife brushed away small tears as she read all the hand written and heartfelt messages about being the greatest Mom on the face of the earth and hearing the kids express just what she means to them.

My seven-year-old daughter made a little booklet in the shape of a bonnet. The idea was to praise Moms for all the different hats they wear. My daughter wrote that my wife was a cook who made great "choclet" chip cookies. She thanked my wife for being a terrific nurse and giving her "medisen" when she needs it. My wife also learned that she's a top-notch sanitation worker because she always tells my daughter that her room is a "pig stie"…which is usually the case.

"I made the scrambled eggs," one son boasted.

"I unwrapped the muffin," another one proudly noted.

"Hey, we have bacon! Cool!" said another one, snatching a slice for himself.

We also gave her a VCR as a gift. It's for the upstairs television. She was getting tired of battling the kids for video time. They're always watching one of their movies or some Pokemon cartoon episode for the millionth time, when she wants to watch "Felicity" from the week before so she can catch up on the latest wacky antics of those whiny, confused college kids. But I digress…

Anyway, the best part of the whole festive day came when the kids broke into a spontaneous rendition of "Happy Mother's Day to You". As the off-key choir struggled to stay together, my wife broke into a very blissful smile. For me, it was one of those moments that you know will be permanently ingrained in your memory. My wife looked pleased and content, watching her children perform for her around the kitchen table. It was one of those extraordinary, mental Kodak moments.

At some point during our corny celebration, I picked up the phone to call my mother to wish her a Happy Mother's Day. I put the kids on first, so that they could speak with their Grandma. A few of them took turns detailing their latest accomplishments and sharing stories about friends my Mom may have met but will never remember.

When I finally had my turn with the phone, I asked if my mother had received the book we sent her, and the gift certificate to the restaurant she enjoys. Fortunately for all concerned, the postal service came through again.

"What's all that noise there?" my mother laughed.

"It's just the kids singing for their Mom," I answered.

What seemed like an uncomfortably long pause followed that. And it was at that instant that I realized my Mom felt lonely. She's lived alone in Pennsylvania since my father died in 1993. She always splits the Thanksgiving, Christmas and New Years holidays between my house and my sister's home in Phoenix. But Mother's Days usually consist of a gift in the mail and a Sunday phone call. We talk about her previous week, the week ahead and what elderly relative is in poor health. That's what happens when careers spread families across the country.

I guess I should have asked, but I wonder how many of those permanently ingrained and cherished Mother's Day memories my Mom has.

When a person is alone on those special days, I'm sure those memories are not enough.

Maybe next year we'll send a colorful bouquet of cardboard flowers and follow it up with a few long-distance songs. That might make for some nice memories to last for a while, at least.

Lessons In Home Improvement.
Lessons In Restraint.

I talk to people about things like grout now. I was never a grout man until recently. Now when I go into other people's homes, I look at their floor tiles and I ask about their grout.

I also check out their cabinets and examine the texture of their stucco. Sometimes I casually count the number of electrical outlets in other people's kitchens. I inquire about other people's sprinkler systems, their water heaters and their landscaping.

I can't stop myself. It's not my fault.

When we bought a new house in Elk Grove our world quickly evolved into something completely the opposite of the way it was. There was a time when I wouldn't give grout the time of day. But buying a home turns you into a whole different type of person. Your perspective changes. You no longer look at a house and just see a house. You see double pane windows and brass light fixtures and cement tile roofs. Even if you try real hard to not let it happen, you cannot stop yourself from looking at a house and dissecting it down to the most basic bits of material.

Speaking of materials, that reminds me that I have to do some comparative shopping for ceiling fans.

Anyway, when I drive through the new neighborhood not only do I slow down to be on guard for small children instinctively chasing after baseballs rolling out onto the streets, but it also gives me a chance to check out other people's landscaping and window coverings. I find myself wondering what types of ground cover people are using and how long they've set the timers on their sprinkler systems. The other day I caught myself nearly coveting another families' trees.

"Hey, that guy's lawn is really green. I wonder if he's a Turfbuilder or a Bandini guy."

The other people living near me need to know: I'm not staring at them, I'm just looking closely at their dwellings.

Please don't be offended. I really wish I could stop myself. Maybe I'll grow out of it with time.

Moving into a new home can be very exciting. But it can also be unnerving because the whole ordeal messes with your mind.

There was a time when I had difficulty going past Border's Books, Barnes and Noble, or some computer store. Now, every time I get within a hundred yards of one of those big home repair palaces my subconscious keeps whispering: "Go ahead! Step inside! They might have a special on grout sealant right now!"

There I go with the grout again.

There was a time when I'd never toss a magazine in the trash. I once had a TIME Magazine and NEWSWEEK collection that would rival any library's periodical section. Now I have stacks and stacks of advertisements from Orchard Supply Hardware—you know, OSH—and The Home Depot. If we get anything from Sears, I'm flipping through it like a high school baseball player studying SPORTS ILLUSTRATED, the swimsuit edition. In fact, my rapidly growing ad collection is getting so large that I might have to construct a special shelf in the garage. Maybe I'll stop by Coast to Coast Hardware and check out shelving.

While I'm there, I should think about a new shovel, maybe a round point shovel with a fiberglass handle. That sounds good.

See what I mean? This has gone beyond a simple preoccupation. And I'm thinking that it might not be too healthy.

The other day, just for grins, I leafed through a bunch of ads and did a mental wish list of things I'd like to buy for the house, and when I added up the total imaginary bill, it was almost equal to the cost of the house itself. It was time for a reality check.

I'm not yet to the point where I can look at bathroom fixtures and tell whether they are Price Pfister, American Standard or Moen, or whether the sinks are pearl onyx, glacier white or dove white, so there still might be hope for me.

But there's a problem. I've got another gallon of grout sealant left over and...

WHERE THE DUST NEVER SETTLES

As I am writing this, the house is finally quiet. It took all day for that to happen. The televisions are silent. The stereos stopped shaking the bedroom walls right after the last "GO TO SLEEP!" rang through the upstairs. No one is crying. No one is wrestling. No one is giggling. No one is even turning the tattered pages of a dog-eared book that is long past due at the school library.

And to be completely honest, I really don't care for it that much. It's like a dismal omen.

Serenity is a rare and strange thing in a house that is so busy that the dust never has a chance to settle. The kinetic energy created by a frenetic family with four growing children keeps the air swirling. Sometimes stopping to take a breath seems like an indulgence.

In our home the typical day starts like a souped up, jet black Porsche in fifth gear and it normally ends like an AMC Pacer—robin egg blue—running out of gas and sputtering to a stop in the driveway. Our house is the palace of perpetual motion. Sometimes I wish that everything would screech to a halt. But that's when I have to snap myself back to reality.

While I enjoy the uncommon quiet, I confess that I don't treasure it as much as I do the commotion. Before too long, when the kids are all away at college or launching their own lives, silence will rule the house. The kid's bedrooms will be empty, like a wing of guestrooms in a suburban bed and breakfast that has a wobbly basketball hoop out in front. The house will always seem tidy because fewer people will be around to leave dirty dishes on end tables and within reach of the dog's thankful tongue. On the plus side, when the kids are gone we'll use less toilet paper. We'll always have plenty of hot water and we'll never run out of bread.

I realize that if the dust ever does settle that would mean the kids have all moved on and that my wife and I are getting on in years. Now, we've already planned to use our long-awaited time together wisely once the children are on their own. My wife and I are even now planning golf lessons, health club memberships, volunteering at church, long walks together and videotaping the grandchildren's school plays. In spite of looking forward to doing those things, I don't look forward to that "getting on" feeling.

If the dust ever does settle it means that the dirty socks—scattered on the living room floor like confetti—are probably mine. It means I'm likely the one who put the milk carton containing three lonely drops back in the refrigerator. It means that the original owners of the cobweb covered basketball trophies and framed report cards are somewhere else, possibly picking up the strewn socks of their own children.

I don't look forward to complete household solitude because it will mean that life is starting to slow down. I fear that when it slows down to a crawl that a full stop is not too far off down the road.

The other day I was driving in my minivan and mentally screaming at the slow moving jerk behind the wheel of the car in front of me. The guy failed to realize that I had places to go. Screaming out loud would only have served as a bad example for the children, so my cursing stayed trapped inside my head.

Move it! The clock is ticking. The meter is running.

Let it run. It's supposed to. As long as the meter is running that means that we are running too.

I welcome living in a house, and living a life where the dust never settles because it means that you are surrounded by spirit and by purpose and by love.

Household noise equals energy. Energy equals vitality. Without consistent clamor, homes become like mausoleums. Besides, silence is overrated any way.

ABOUT THE AUTHOR

Tim Herrera is an author, columnist, and award winning journalist and public speaker living in Elk Grove, California. His first collection of essays titled *"I'm Their Dad! Not Their Babysitter!"* was published in May 2000 by Writers Club Press.

From 1995 to 2002 Tim wrote the weekly PERSPECTIVE column that appears in the ELK GROVE/LAGUNA issue of THE SACRAMENTO BEE.

Tim retired from coaching recreational league sports such as soccer and baseball after coming to the realization that he has limited knowledge to pass onto young players. He currently spends a lot of time cheering on the sidelines of soccer games and in the bleachers at basketball games to the point that other parents connected with his children's teams are reluctant to sit near him.

During his professional journalism career, Tim has worked in such markets as Sacramento, Dallas and Pittsburgh. Tim has served as a communications director, radio news director, television and radio news reporter, talk show host and writer. He is the recipient of more than a dozen journalism awards. He has written articles for nationally distributed publications including THE NEW YORK TIMES SALES SYNDICATE, MODERN DAD MAGAZINE, NEWS PHOTOGRAPHER MAGAZINE and CATHOLIC FORESTER. His work has also appeared in cyber magazines, including *Real Families* and *My Village*.

Tim has been married since 1984 to his wife, Carol, a kindergarten teacher and is the father of four children, Nick, Mark, Ben and Amy. They serve as a great source of writing material and comfort.

You can e-mail Tim at thedadof4@yahoo.com.

0-595-21452-5

www.ingramcontent.com/pod-product-compliance
Lightning Source LLC
Chambersburg PA
CBHW020916290526
45784CB00002BA/577